# The stimulus factor

**FINANCIAL TIMES**

Prentice Hall

In an increasingly competitive world, it is quality
of thinking that gives an edge – an idea that opens new
doors, a technique that solves a problem, or an insight
that simply helps make sense of it all.

We work with leading authors in the fields of
management and finance to bring cutting-edge thinking
and best learning practice to a global market.

Under a range of leading imprints, including
*Financial Times Prentice Hall*, we create world-class
print publications and electronic products giving readers
knowledge and understanding which can then be
applied, whether studying or at work.

To find out more about our business and professional
products, you can visit us at www.business-minds.com

For other Pearson Education publications, visit
www.pearsoned-ema.com

Pearson
Education

# The stimulus factor

The new dimension in motivation

## David Freemantle

FINANCIAL TIMES
Prentice Hall

*An imprint of* **Pearson Education**

London / New York / San Francisco / Toronto / Sydney / Tokyo / Singapore
Hong Kong / Cape Town / Madrid / Paris / Milan / Munich / Amsterdam

PEARSON EDUCATION LIMITED

Head Office:
Edinburgh Gate
Harlow CM20 2JE
Tel: +44 (0)1279 623623
Fax: +44 (0)1279 431059

London Office:
128 Long Acre
London WC2E 9AN
Tel: +44 (0)20 7447 2000
Fax: +44 (0)20 7240 5771
Website: www.business-minds.com

First published in Great Britain in 2001

The right of David Freemantle
to be identified as author
of this work has been asserted by him in accordance
with the Copyright, Designs and Patents Act 1988.

ISBN 0 273 64994 9

*British Library Cataloguing in Publication Data*
A CIP catalogue record for this book can be obtained from the British Library.

10 9 8 7 6 5 4 3 2 1

Typeset by Northern Phototypesetting Co. Ltd, Bolton
Printed and bound in Great Britain by Biddles Ltd, Guildford & King's Lynn

*The Publishers' policy is to use paper manufactured from sustainable forests.*

*To the latest all-smiling addition*
*to the Freemantle family,*
*my granddaughter*
*Molly Kate*

# About the author

**Dr David Freemantle** gained his doctorate at London University before becoming a production manager with Mars Ltd. He had a meteoric career progression culminating with a position on the board of British Caledonian Airways. In 1985 he founded his own company, Superboss Ltd, which specializes in the areas of motivation, leadership and customer service. He travels the world speaking at conferences and running seminars and has gained an international reputation for his thought-provoking talks and programs. His clients include major airlines, retail chains, banks and government organizations. This is David's tenth book. His previous books have been published in 17 different languages and include *What Customers Like About You* (Nicholas Brealey, 1998) and *80 Things You Must Do To Be A Great Boss* (McGraw-Hill, 1995). He lives in Windsor with his wife Mechi, daughter Ruth-Elena and step-daughter Linnet. He can be contacted at: team@superboss.co.uk

# Contents

# Acknowledgments

I am exceptionally grateful to a large number of people who have contributed to this book. My wife Mechi, as ever, provided much encouragement including the stimulus of some invigorating discussions as the book evolved. She was ably supported by my daughter Ruth-Elena and my stepdaughter Linnet Armengol as we explored many contentious issues over the dinner table. My eldest daughter Kate was also instrumental in arranging some of the fascinating interviews for me whilst my eldest son Tom and his wife Nicky sought to divert my attention by producing a second grandchild during the period of writing.

The team of FT Prentice Hall, led by Richard Stagg, aided and abetted by such stars as Penelope Allport and Angela Lewis, also provided invaluable guidance. I was impressed by their professional approach.

I am very thankful to a number of organizations that gave me the freedom to meet their managers and employees and were happy for these people to say whatever they liked in terms of motivation and demotivation. These companies included Austin Reed, Bank Atlantic (USA), Beijing Gong Ti Yu Tai Sports Company (China), Carnival Cruises (USA), Conrad Hilton Hotels (Singapore), Equitable Life Assurance Society, Hallmark Cards (USA), Hilton Hotels, HSBC Bank, NatWest Bank, ReedPrint, Ritz Carlton Hotels (Singapore), the Royal Borough of Windsor and Maidenhead, Saatchi & Saatchi, Schering-Plough, Starbucks (Singapore), WPA Health Care Insurance and the Virgin Group. Furthermore many participants at my seminars with organizations such as the Child Support Agency, Fairview Homes and Singapore Airlines Terminal Services (SATS) presented valuable points on 'what motivated them'.

Much of the substance of this book evolves from the wisdom of the large number of people I interviewed and the valuable insights they gave me into their own personal motivations. I am most appreciative of the time they devoted to me and their openness and honesty in revealing their innermost thoughts and feelings. Many of the interviewees prefer to remain anonymous. However, I am particularly indebted to the following people: Tony Ager, David Askwith, Becky, Belardo, Sir Michael Bichard, Geoff Biscoe, Paul Bondon, Reuben Braddock, Claire Brand, Sir Richard Branson, Peter Bridges, Keith Brown, Tony Burton, Gerry Busk, Jean Carvalho, Kevin Chappenden, Dr Liz Clark, Nick Clayton, Brian Clegg, Claire Cornish, David Chu, Bob Dickinson, Helen Downey, Richard Fannon, Andrew Fisher, Sanchia Gallifent, Christine Gan, Emma Gill, Joe Gillick, Jonathan Goss, Terry Gould, Heinrich Grafe, Lisa Greaves, Arnie Harmsworth, Davina Hardiman, Deanna Hawkins, Clive Hearn, Adam Hiscock, Alex Huang, Debbie Huffman, Sandy Hughes, Adrian Humphreys, Ee Tiang Hwee, John-Paul Jenkins, Ali Jones, Linda Jones, Sarah Jones, Joe Kadiri, Andrew Keitch, Richard Killoran, Jackie King, Julia Kundomal, Michael Lee, David Leo, Gael Lindenfield, Stuart Lindenfield, Brian Longstreet, Viv Lye, Gordon McKenzie, Mario Macari, Tracy Manning, Colin Marvell, Jackie Matthews, Stephen Millard, Tanya Pillay Nair, Lisa O'Brien, Kate Ogunbanke, Dafydd Owen, Steve Pendray, David Palmer, Elena Riu, Adrian Schuler, Joy Senneck, Howard Shelley, Becky South, Melinda Still, Phil Stone, Jules Szwarzak, Mark Tyler, Alan Westwell, Kim Ward, Clare Wheadon, Kelly Whitehouse, David Wilmot, Jessica Zhang Yuan, Rona Jing Zhang.

To be *effective* you must factor a **stimulus** into everything you do

when customers buy
when employees perform
when companies succeed
**is when the stimulus factor is at work**

all movement results from a stimulus
all motivation results from a stimulus
all types of performance result from a stimulus
**all our behaviors, actions, communications and
decisions result from our responses to stimuli**

how to stimulate your customers to buy?
how to stimulate your employees to perform?
how to stimulate success?
**how to get the stimulus factor to work?**

we have to change the **stimulus** to change *behavior*

**the stimulus factor at work**
is the mind at work
the heart at work
the soul at work
as well as the body at work

it is not enough to have needs and wants
it is not enough to prioritize those needs and wants
**those needs and wants have to be stimulated**

to be **stimulating** is to be *thought-provoking* and ...

... inspirational and entertaining and lively and
vibrant and colorful and appreciative and trusting
and ambitious and creative and imaginative and
exciting and fascinating and dynamic and incisive
and motivating and encouraging and compelling
and understanding and challenging and innovative

to succeed we need to relate as well as to reason
to relate we need to feel as well as to think
to feel we need to work from the heart as well as
from the mind
**to work from the heart we need to stimulate
positive emotions as well as positive thoughts**

every single thing a manager does or says
at work is a stimulus
and people respond accordingly
this book aims to help you understand these stimuli
and to motivate people to respond accordingly

this book aims to be a **stimulus** to your *personal success*

# 1

# The stimulus factor at work

High performance is not just a function of energy,
skill, experience, talent and knowledge but also a function
of the stimulus factor at work.

## The stimulus factor and high performance

In the absence of a frequent stimulus your organization will fail. Success in business arises from the way companies stimulate customers in a chosen marketplace and stimulate employees to perform for those customers. When an effective stimulus is not provided relationships atrophy and a business will go into decline. Therefore a stimulus must be factored into all business relationships whether with customers, employees or suppliers.

There are many parallels in life. For example, should you fail to stimulate your body with exercise it will grow flabby and eventually become diseased. Should you fail to stimulate your mind with new thoughts then it will close in on itself and you will become a bore, not only to others but also to yourself. Should you fail to stimulate your heart with positive feelings then it will become clogged with progressive layers of negativity and you will become a miserable old sourpuss who feels so bad you make everyone feel bad. Should you fail to stimulate your soul with freshly discovered wisdom then you will lose your spirit and become inhuman.

The same principle applies to the workplace. Should you fail periodically to stimulate the motivation of the people in your team their performance will progressively deteriorate. Similarly when it comes to the very essence of selling should you fail to stimulate your customers with refreshing new experiences they will become tired with your company and its products and take their business elsewhere.

Stimulus deprivation leads to the atrophy of the vital energies that employees need to perform and customers need to buy. High performance is not just a function of energy, skill, experience, talent and knowledge, but it is also a function of the *stimulus factor* at work.

Equal to the problem of stimulus deprivation is that of stimulus saturation. The solution is to strike a balance in which an optimum set of stimuli is harnessed to spark the motivation of employees to perform well and of customers to make choices in your favor. It is through applying the stimulus factor that this balance can be attained.

## The world of ever increasing stimulation

In today's world drudgery is out and stimulation has become an essential need. Life, together with hard work, is becoming less of a boring chore but more a roller-coaster ride through a thousand interrupts. We live in a world of ever increasing stimulation, where people are ceaselessly bombarded with stimuli every moment of the day whilst at the same time they are desperate to seek new thrills to sustain their motivation. Paradoxically, stimulus saturation turns to non-stimulating numbness very quickly. We can have too much of it.

> Drudgery is out, stimulation is in

The golden stimulus of silence and personal space is rapidly being displaced by the frenetic stimulus of interference and intrusion. We have become uncomfortable with silence and the sound of ourselves. Increasing numbers of people cannot even walk down the street without a phone stuck to their ears. Adrenalin and hyperactivity have become the norms whilst serotonin and serenity are assigned to the realms of nostalgia and early retirement.

In our e-world of e-commerce, e-mail, the internet, mobile phones, pagers, DVD, television channels by the hundred, together with interactive TV, we have no hope of blocking out all these stimuli and the millions of advertisements and influence-seeking messages that seek to motivate us every day. We have to learn to be effective in the way we manage them: whether that be by the way we transmit them or by the way we receive them.

What we cannot do is avoid them. Stimulus management and striking the balance as appropriate will become the order of the day.

# Stimulus: the missing dimension of motivation

Perversely, the transmission and receipt of stimuli is essential for the very process of motivation. Stimulus is the missing third dimension in all theories of motivation. Each of the needs in Maslow's hierarchy has to be stimulated to be met. The internal stimulus of a hunger pain or the external stimulus of the smell of fresh bread will move us towards satisfying our needs for food.

To motivate customers to buy and employees to perform, a stimulus must be factored into interactions with them. In the absence of such a stimulus both motivation and performance will erode and people will progressively revert to habit and routine. When this happens their minds close down and they go about their daily business in automatic mode, thinking what they have thought before, buying what they have always bought and working in the same old time-honored ways. Companies relying on these well-drilled thinking processes and behaviors put themselves at immense risk as competitors move in to stimulate the marketplace. The challenge of competition is to open people's hearts and minds to the possibilities of fresh ideas and fresh experiences. Similarly, organizations have to be stimulated if they are to retain their competitive edge and this means having managers at all levels who have the ability to stimulate people.

> To motivate customers to buy and employees to perform, a stimulus must be factored into interactions with them

## External and internal stimuli

To perform at work employees need both external and internal stimuli. Without these people do not work. Traditionally these stimuli have been negative or, to be more exact, based on fear. One such internal fear is of having one's family go hungry and not providing a roof over their heads. This fear is a powerful emotional stimulus to work.

A reciprocal external fear is the threat of punishment and thus of losing one's job – whether it be for making a mistake or alienating one's boss. Such fears have always provided a powerful stimulus to please one's bosses (or to perform, as it is nowadays called). These traditions remain in most organizations today, although their senior executives would in all probability deny it. Such is the delusion that remains when it comes to matters of motivation, creativity, trust, customer service and business relationships in general.

A progressive minority of company managers create an array of positive stimuli for their employees to ignite their motivation and to help them to perform exceptionally well. Most executives, however, still inadvertently or deliberately generate negative stimuli, which demoralize employees and alienate customers.

## The stimulus paradox

As human beings we are full of paradoxes – of light and dark, of good and bad, and of conflicting needs. Success cannot be experienced without failure, pleasure without pain, happiness without sadness, love without hate. And similarly with our desperate need for stimulation. At one level we don't want it but at the next level we are desperate for it. At one level we are desperate for comfort and security – for a life in which all our worries have disappeared and we 'can tick over quite nicely' without thinking about where the next slice of bread (or vacation in the sun) is going to come from. Actually the prospect (and possibly the reality) of a vacation in the sun is a stimulus. If and when we achieve continuous comfort and security we quickly become bored with it and desperate for a stimulus of some kind. It might be a fantasy to lie in bed all day Sunday, but in practice the benefit of the comfort gradually disappears (normally around midday) and we become desperate for something different – for a fresh stimulus, for a chat with our friends, for a brief shopping expedition, for a trip to the cinema, for a game of football, for a vacation in the sun.

It is almost as if we are never satisfied with the pleasures of the present and are always seeking future delights. Tomorrow's reality rarely matches the fantasy we hold of it, yet it is our fantasy that acts as vital stimulus for future movement.

# The stimulus factor at work for customers

The stimulus factor has immense implications for the way we relate to customers and serve them. It is much too simplistic to assert that customer choice is based on a set of rational factors such as price, product specification, quality, service, location and reputation. Purchasing decisions also result from responses to the ways companies stimulate their customers. The best companies reach into their customers' souls and become their soulmates by stimulating and establishing vital emotional connections. These companies create genuine meaning in their customers' lives. For example, the best retailers aim to stimulate their customers' interest, to open up vistas of fascinating new experiences, to create additional value for them and therefore increase the esteem of those who purchase their products.

## Commerce and the stimulus factor

In fact, the whole world of commerce is driven by the stimulus factor, or at least 99.9 per cent of it. Most companies would be out of business tomorrow if the sole reason people bought things was to satisfy their basic physical needs for simple nutrition, rudimentary clothing, heat and light and a roof over their heads. Who really needs superstores stocking 40 types of mineral water and vast ranges of exotic fruits with fancy names? Who needs expensive restaurants or inexpensive fast food joints? Who needs a microwave or a mobile telephone? Who needs fashion? Who needs most of the things you find in the stores today as advertised in the papers yesterday? Who needs vacations?

> The whole world of commerce is driven by the stimulus factor

Actually we all do. We all need stimulation in order to survive. The reason people go shopping, go on vacations, participate in or watch sport, and seek out various entertainments is because stimulation is essential to life.

## The stimulating shopping experience

Here I am sitting drinking coffee in a food court in the rather large Sawgrass shopping mall in Florida and writing this whilst watching people stroll by. Why are all these people here visiting this shopping mall? Is it to spend a few cents on a crust of bread or possibly a little more on a smidgen of meat? Is it to buy some cheap clothes to replace their rags? In fact I don't see any rags. Are they here to meet their basic physicals needs? The answer is obvious. No! Most people visiting shopping malls could meet their basic physical needs with 5 per cent of their income.

## Our deep-rooted psychological need for stimulation

But these people *are* here to have another need satisfied – the need for stimulation. Most people in our modern society are beyond surviving at subsistence level. Our basic needs are well met and almost taken for granted. I suspect that most readers of this book have little experience of struggling for a crust of bread, a coat to keep them warm and a bed to lie on.

However, if our basic physical needs are well met, do we have any further physical needs? Do we have real physical needs for avocado pears, kiwi fruit, Chinese cuisine and vacations on paradise islands? Do we have real physical needs to see the latest Simpsons' episode or listen to the latest single by Britney Spears (or whoever is in fashion). And why do we have fashions that change every few months? What is the point?

The point is that we need stimulating. We need something different all the time. We need to have our senses excited and our imaginations stretched. It is our souls, spirits and emotions that need stimulating. Stimulation is a basic human need.

People need to have their imaginations stimulated by eye-catching windows displays, by new products being promoted and by the prospect of tempting, money-saving bargains. The experience of shopping is a fantasy world in which people visualize what the future might bring for them. The wide variety of stimuli helps them convert fragments of these fantasies into fleeting realities as they make the occasional purchase.

> We need to have our senses excited and our imaginations stretched

Who needs more than two pairs of shoes? Who needs more than two suits? Who needs perfume, jewelry and platinum pens? At the level of our most basic physical needs, nobody does. However, when it comes to our psychological needs, everyone does.

Most people have a deep-rooted psychological need for stimulation. One way this need can be met is by shopping – by gazing into windows, by browsing, by touching and examining more closely things they are unlikely ever to possess. To quote Paco Underhill (1999): "We use shopping as therapy, reward, bribery, pastime, as an excuse to get out of the house, as a way to troll for potential loved ones, as entertainment, as a form of education or even worship, as a way to kill time."

Only occasionally on their visits to shopping malls do people buy things they really need, for example new school uniforms for the kids. Are uniforms a need? No and yes! School uniforms are just a social psychological need added to a basic need.

People come shopping at this mall to benefit from a complex range of stimuli: they come for the ambience, the lights, the colors, the live piano music, the smells (perfume, coffee, burgers) and the sight of other people strolling around. They are here to obtain experiences of shopping which they can articulate as personal stories to stimulate conversation with their families, friends and neighbors back home. "I just loved that new Armani outfit they had in the window!" "Did you see the price of that new digital television!" "They've just opened a new electronics store on the second level." "I didn't like that lady who served us in the card-shop, she was most offhand!"

## The need for stimulus at work

And whilst customers go shopping to be stimulated (in addition to making purchases to meet their basic physical needs), the research for this book confirmed that people go to work for the same reason: for the stimulus of activity, of actually doing something as opposed to doing nothing. In addition to meeting their basic physical needs for wages, they also go to work for the stimulus of enhanced personal esteem, of social interaction, of individual achievement, of identification with the company ideals and successes. Fun, gossip, laughter, *esprit de corps* and variety of activity are other stimulus factors that come into play, as well as escape from the perceived drudgery of home.

As soon as you get a job – and as long as you do it properly – you can take it for granted that you are going to get paid. Pay ceases to become an effective stimulus once you're in a job. To quote Geoff Biscoe, a sales manager with a print company and one of the people I interviewed as part of the research:

I've been paid many different ways over the years, sometimes with a straight salary and other times with a variety of bonus or commission schemes. In the end it works out to the same thing. I still get paid the same in the end. It doesn't affect my approach. I still approach customers the same way. I can't put on more airs and graces just because there's a new incentive scheme.

Most jobs are based on routines prescribed by bosses and as such risk becoming boring. "I could do this job with my eyes shut!" To alleviate boredom, people create their own stimuli, which can have an either positive or negative impact on their results. The best bosses recognize this and therefore work hard in partnership with their teams to create those stimuli that have a positive impact on performance.

A couple of weeks have passed since I wrote the above paragraphs and I am now back in the UK. It is early morning and I am sitting in a small café called Stockpot in London's West End eating breakfast prior to a meeting along the road. A couple of street cleaners come in for their bacon, egg, toast and tea. They joke with the two waitresses whom they obviously know. Then the cleaners' boss comes in and they joke with him too. He sits down with them and points to something in the tabloid newspaper he's carrying.

> The best bosses work hard in partnership with their teams to create those stimuli that have a positive impact on performance

They laugh. A couple of traffic wardens come in and order some coffee to take out. Whilst waiting they chat to the waitresses preparing their coffee and then turn to pass some comments to the street cleaners about last night's football.

Is any of this work? Are these people motivated? Why do these people come to this particular café as opposed to the 20 others within a short radius? And why do I choose this café, as I invariably do? Is it for the excellent food, is it for the price of the food? Or is it for something else?

Whichever way you look at the above scene you will find a stimulus factored into the work the various people are doing – whether they be waitresses, street cleaners, traffic wardens or business consultants like me. I go to this café not only for a great breakfast but because I like the way the waitresses treat me, that is the stimulus. The same applies to the other customers. The street cleaners and traffic wardens are motivated by the stimulus of a brief social interaction with each other as well as with the waitresses. Being out in the wind and the rain looking after the streets of London is well worth the effort when there is an additional stimulus of a visit to a café you like. Hard work has to be supplemented with the occasional stimulus in order to sustain motivation.

## The myth of scientific management

The emphasis on a scientific and rational approach to management has led to the neglect of such unscientific areas as the soul, spirit and emotion and the power they have in determining the fate of any enterprise. Frequently employees lose their souls to their employers. Employees become cogs in a giant organization machine that grinds on and on. Such organizations effectively dehumanize their employees, giving scant regard to their souls, spirits and emotions (all of which need to be stimulated at work). Regrettably, such organizations dehumanize their customers too. When customers detect this they defect if they can.

As mentioned above we are bombarded with stimuli all the time. It would be wrong to say that we cannot escape such bombardment. In fact we all do – we just block out those stimuli that we do not want to stimulate us. Our souls, in conjunction with our brains, are working subconsciously all the time on the selection process we continually deploy to let in desired stimuli and block out undesired stimuli.

## The art of business management

The art of business management, whether sparking customer choice or motivating employees, is to open up the stimulus-blocking defences that all human beings build up during a life time. To do this requires stimulating our desires, our wants and our needs and then helping fulfil them. This in turn requires immense powers of understanding of people, whether they be customers, suppliers, employees or colleagues.

What do people really desire, want and need (at work or at home) when buying things or doing things? To obtain the necessary answers requires not only a deep understanding of their attitudes, behaviors and emotions but also reaching into and stimulating their souls and spirits.

The definition of what people desire, want and need does not and can never conform to a formula, or a number of formal logics, or a set of scientifically analyzed factors. Such formulae tend to assume a prescribed set of customer and employee behaviors that will result in responses to specified commercial and management activities. Such is the myth of modern scientific management. As soon as you attempt to reduce business and motivation to a set of formulae you effectively dehumanize people, treating them as robots who are compelled to move by well-defined mechanisms (procedures, policies, regulations, systems etc.).

> To discover what people want we have to reach into and stimulate their souls and spirits

Each person on this planet has a unique set of desires, wants and needs that are continually evolving, changing and being re-prioritized. These desires, wants and needs are a reflection of an individual's personal identity and self. As such they grow and develop by the day. I am not the same person I was yesterday: since then I have learnt something new, become a little wiser, acquired a slightly different attitude on specific issues and basically grown my 'self' a fraction more. My needs will have changed from yesterday and therefore my priorities too. The closer a company can get to a person's individual self then the better position it will be in to discover whether it can meet that person's wants and needs.

## Wants and needs for stimulation

There is a fine line between a want and a need. We *need* food but we *want* tasty food. People both want and need stimulation. A 'want' does not have to be met, whilst a need must be met. A need is absolute. For most of us, we do not need all the food we eat, but without any food at all we die.

Social welfare departments around the world struggle all the time with the definition of needs in relation to wants. An immobile bed-ridden old person might need physical help from a carer (lifting, cleaning, making beds, feeding), but will in all probability also want the stimulus of social contact with the carer in terms of chit-chat and a friendly relationship. Where do you draw the line in terms of provision? Where do you put the time? Into addressing the needs only or into the wants as well?

A customer might need to buy a new washing machine but also might want to spend half an hour telling the store assistant a long complicated saga about what went wrong with the previous model. The purchase of a washing machine might be stimulated by a basic need (to wash clothes), although the washing machine is not a need in itself (clothes can always be washed by hand). The visit to the store provides essential stimuli that take the customer out of the boredom of his or her everyday routine. On arrival at the store there are many displays to stimulate the eye, there is much interesting information to be gleaned and there are studies to be made between competitive products and the bargains to be had. There is also the potential of some stimulating social contact (with the store assistant) from which to benefit. On returning home the experience of purchasing a washing machine provides an opportunity to stimulate family relationships with a fascinating story.

In the above example there are four types of stimulus at work in motivating the customer to buy. The first is a basic stimulus (the need to keep clean), the second is an aspirational stimulus (the aim of acquiring a new washing machine), the third is a diversionary stimulus (the enjoyment of the actual shopping experience), whilst the fourth stimulus is social (obtaining stories to tell families and friends back home). These four types of stimulus are drawn from the 17 clusters of stimuli that are the subject of Chapter 3.

Thus there is a wide range of stimuli at work in the process of purchasing a washing machine. It is not just simply a buying transaction. The stimuli that work will vary from one customer to another depending on their individual wants and needs. Successful retailers are those who create sufficient stimuli to attract customers in pursuit of fulfilling their specific wants and needs.

> The art of business management is to create the stimuli people want and need in order to move in the desired direction for all concerned

As we are constantly bombarded with stimuli we select only those we want and need and then act accordingly. The art of business management is to create the stimuli people want and need in order to move in the desired direction for all concerned.

## Putting the stimulus factor to work

The business managers who tend to be successful nowadays are those who are able to apply the stimulus factor in motivating customers to buy and employees to perform. Customers will not move towards you and purchase your products unless you put the stimulus factor to work. To stimulate your profits you have to find additional ways of stimulating your customers to buy from you. Equally, you have to find additional ways of stimulating employees to work and perform for you. Pay alone is not enough – it is only one of a range of stimuli that can have a positive or negative impact on employees.

### The stimulus of traditional retailing vs. e-commerce

The advent of e-commerce and the additional competitive pressures it places on traditional retailing make the application of the stimulus factor essential. People love the stimulus of the internet and the ability to browse and search for product information; they love the wide range of choices available, the discounted prices and the ability to make purchases in their own time and at their own pace. To overcome the restrictions of retail (restricted opening hours, distance from home, slow service, limited product offerings, high prices), stores are having to provide additional stimuli to attract customers to them.

For example, whilst **www.amazon.com** is offering over 2.5 million books for sale on the internet, each at a discounted price, retail booksellers like Barnes & Noble, Borders and Waterstone's (in the UK) are opening up huge bookstores. Thus Waterstone's has opened up a six-floor bookstore in

Piccadilly, London, within a couple of minutes' walk of two of their major competitors. Kinokuniya has opened a vast bookstore in the Ngee Ann City shopping mall in Singapore. Why open up huge bookstores when anyone can buy a book more cheaply on the internet at a more convenient time and in a more convenient place (your home)? The answer relates to the stimulus factor at work.

## The stimulating purchasing experience

Some might argue that a book is a book is a book and it doesn't matter where you buy it. However, adding to the value of the book is the experience of purchasing it and it is this experience that needs to be stimulated to attract customers to you. Thus at Waterstone's in Piccadilly the experience is stimulated not only by the excellent displays and the sense of space but also by the availability of a restaurant, a juice bar and a coffee shop, as well as large tables at which one can sit and browse. The process of purchasing a book can be turned into a stimulating experience to be enjoyed for a couple of hours with the family, or during a short half-hour break from the exigencies of the office routine. At the Kinokuniya bookstore in Singapore a stimulus is offered not only through two attractive coffee shops, the instant availability of a huge range of books in Chinese, English and other European languages, the helpful staff, but also in relatively minor aspects such as the attractive and distinctive carrier bags that you will not find elsewhere. At the Barnes & Noble store in Plantation, Florida, a stimulus is offered by regular book readings and a range of events to add value to the experience of purchasing books at the store.

And so to a prime stimulant, coffee. Until a few years ago you could purchase that stimulant in a grocery store to take home and brew yourself, or alternatively you could drink it in a café where the choice was simple: black or white, with or without sugar. Some might argue that coffee is coffee is coffee and it doesn't matter how you consume it, it is still the same caffeine stimulant that will give you your fix. Walk into any Starbucks store and you will realize that the world of coffee has moved on. The stimulant can now be purchased and consumed in a wide range of stimulating ways. You can even purchase it with the stimulant taken out! The range has become the stimulus – whether you like Kenyan, Arabic or decaffeinated beans to take home, or whether you like (to drink in or take out) short, tall or grande espresso, Americano, caffe latte, caffe mocho, cappucino or frappucino, with or without a range of heavenly syrups and or cream. The wide choice is stimulating, the ambience is stimulating, the food products on offer are stimulating. Coffee is no longer a simple stimulant which gives you a fix, it is now at the core of a stimulating experience which goes beyond the coffee itself. And so with books, clothes, grocery products, insurance, banking, travel and virtually everything you need to purchase in your life.

For example, some might argue that travel companies are solely interested in transporting people from A to B. After all, a seven-hour flight is a seven-hour flight. The world of travel has moved on. Now we have a variety of in-flight meals, hot towels, seats with built-in videos, kiddies' play-packs, showers on arrival and comfortable lounges on departure.

Even a visit to the cinema is evidence of the stimulus factor at work. The world of cinema has moved on. At cinemas around the world there are now 'premier screens' which offer you the facility of relaxing in a comfortable lounge prior to the performance, indulging in a little alcoholic refreshment, together with some free crudités and popcorn. Why bother to watch the video at home a year later when you can see the film now in an environment which stimulates your sense of luxury and well-being?

## Extreme stimuli

The film itself is a supreme stimulus and in these liberal times film makers strive to shock us more and more with stimuli that a few years ago would have been totally impermissible. As people become saturated by the thrills and titillation of what was once forbidden they now seek stimulus extremes that go beyond many people's boundaries. In 1999 one of the most successful films around was *The Blair Witch Project*, an inexpensively produced film that relied on the simple stimulus of fear and shock to entertain people. The paradox is that many people love negative stimuli – they love the sight of violence on the screens, they love to be frightened to death and they love to take risks.

In an article in *Time Magazine* Karl Taro Greenfeld (1999) wrote: "Heading into the millennium, America has embarked on a national orgy of thrill seeking and risk taking." He cites the rising popularity of extreme sports such as snowboarding, ice climbing and paragliding, as well the way an increasing number of Americans speculate on the stock exchange. A month later in the same magazine an article entitled "Shock for shock's sake" described the outrage at certain exhibits in a show of young British artists in the Brooklyn Museum of Art. The show's theme was "Sensation" and included an exhibit of a black Madonna festooned with elephant dung.

These are extremes in our world of stimulation. We might not like the stimuli – we might even find them morally offensive – but the harsh reality is that they exist and the reason they exist is that there is a minority of people who crave for such extremes. Damien Hirst's dissected animals are not for me, but for others they are a lure. Who am I to judge? Furthermore, I quickly turn the page when I see one of Benetton's advertisements depicting the misery of AIDS victims or refugees. To quote Jesper Kunde (2000): "Benetton is a strong Concept Brand. But for how long? There is a thorough lack of consequence in the things the company does."

> The transmission and receipt of stimuli has to be managed to achieve a desired effect

## The management of stimuli

In other words, transmitting extreme stimuli just for the sake of it is pointless. We might as well run along the street shouting obscenities. The transmission and receipt of stimuli has to be managed to achieve a desired response – and that management process is far more subtle and complex than just using and abusing the extremes of civil acceptability.

In stimulating the motivation of customers to buy and employees to perform, we therefore have to accept that within ever widening boundaries of acceptance there is an increasing range of stimuli to draw upon.

# The ultimate stimulus: human behavior

The ultimate stimulant is human behavior and all the thinking, feeling and spirit that drives it. This has special significance in the world of work where traditionally a job had little to do with human behavior. Until recent times employees were hired to expend physical energy in undertaking specific tasks and that would be the nature of the work for which they were paid. Employees were seen as instruments of labor in a mechanical process of using human energy to convert raw materials into saleable goods. As long as the task was performed, behavior had little to do with it. The smile was irrelevant.

The world of work has moved on. Now the smile is essential. No longer are you expected just to work but you are also expected to behave in a way that is consistent with company requirements. You are expected to exhibit behaviors that not only your customers like but that your colleagues like too.

In addition to your work of cleaning tables, or answering telephones, or fixing crashed computers, you are expected to treat your customers, internal or external, in a special type of way. Nowadays waiters and waitresses have to serve people in addition to serving food, telephonists have to respond to people rather than answer telephones, whilst service engineers are expected to fix people's problems with equipment as opposed to merely fixing equipment. This holistic approach to service and business means having to find a range of new stimuli to create the relationships customers desire.

## The story of the squashed apple

One of the people interviewed for this book, David Wilmot, Customer Relations Manager with The Equitable Life Assurance Society, tells a story of how a customer telephoned one day with a query about an insurance claim. The call was constantly interrupted by the customer who kept breaking off to shout at a child who was screaming in the background. "What's going on there?" asked the claims agent. "Oh! My three-year-old is just treading an apple into the carpet" replied the customer. Later, when the claims agent wrote to the customer, she mentioned the apple incident in the letter. The customer was duly appreciative of the sensitive and caring response. Whilst most people would have ignored this stimulus (kid screaming in the background) this agent seized the opportunity to add a positive stimulus to a routine response to a routine enquiry and thus "humanize" the relationship. The task was to respond to a claim, the behavior was to stimulate a relationship with the customer.

> The stimulus factor has a major impact on every aspect of the way a business operates

Wherever you look in the world of business, companies are moving away from solely conducting mechanistic, financially measured transactions with customers to the provision of a total experience that transcends the simple supply–purchase equation. This is the stimulus factor at work and it has a major impact on every aspect of the way a business operates, especially in relation to the nature of the management task itself.

## The stimulating task of a manager

Like all other aspects of business operations, the manager's task has moved on. Traditionally a manager's task was to get a job done on time, to defined standards, with minimal cost and using an absolute minimum number of people. A manager administered the process of converting the raw materials into saleable goods for as little cost as possible. That was it. People were defined as costs and it was the costs that had to be managed. Many companies still operate that way today. Cost reduction is the major stimulus that drives these businesses (eventually out of business!).

In progressive companies, employees are no longer seen as costly commodities to be minimized in the interests of productivity and profitability. Instead, employees form part of a working community that needs to be continually stimulated in order to survive. This working community, the company, ideally has a set of interests, beliefs and values that are shared by every person involved with it. It is these interests, beliefs and values that provide an essential stimulus to the experience of employment. The role of managers is to stimulate the various teams within this working community, to sustain their interest, their goodwill and thus optimize their performance in meeting the needs of the evolving market within which they conduct their business.

> One or more stimuli have to be factored into everything you do in your business

Wherever you look you will find companies that are out-competing their rivals by putting the stimulus factor to work – whether it is insurance companies like WPA Medical Care (UK), The Equitable Life Assurance Society (UK) or Progressive Insurance (USA), all of whom aim to help (as opposed to hinder) customers making insurance claims; or banks like Bank Atlantic (USA) or HSBC (UK), who similarly go out of their way to help customers. Help for customers is an essential stimulus and falls within the cluster of altruistic stimuli, which will be referred to later (*see* Chapter 3).

## Applying the stimulus factor to everything you do

In summary, the stimulus factor is a critical albeit neglected dimension in the motivation of customers and employees. It means that one or more stimuli have to be factored into everything you do in your business to ensure its profitability and success. It means that you have to stimulate your customers to buy and your employees to perform and that you have to provide an overall stimulating environment in which business transactions and work take place. It means that you have to seek out stimulating ways of hiring stimulating people who can stimulate the interest of potential and existing customers, as well as come up with stimulating new ideas. It means that you have to provide frequent stimuli to your employees to perform, for example by providing them with stimulating training and development. It means that your reward system has to be stimulating (and it will be argued later that one of the least stimulating rewards is a financial one). It means that you have to have managers who know how to stimulate employees and it means that you will have to excel in the application of language and imagination as a stimulus. All these are issues that will be addressed in the pages that follow.

## Become a stimulating person

Most importantly, it means that you, the reader, must learn how to become a stimulating person. You will need to learn how to stimulate yourself as well as others and then sustain high levels of stimulation. Chapter 5 is devoted to this topic.

# The stimulus factor and motivation

Stimulation, whilst closely linked to motivation, is not the same as motivation. The latter is all to do with motives and movement ("this is the reason I move in this direction"). Stimulation relates to the initial spark that ignites the expenditure of energy in moving in a desired direction. It relates to the original source of any human behavior, whether external (environment or another person's behavior) or internal (our innermost thoughts, feelings and spirit).

As will be explained in the coming chapters, the provision of an essential stimulus is not simply the product of a conscious reasoning process, no matter how rational it appears to be, but is also heavily influenced by the heart and the soul. Traditionally, managers have sought out a logical set of "motivators" that can be applied mechanistically to employees to sustain and improve performance. It is this mechanistic approach (using external "motivators") that limits most approaches to motivation. Applying the "stimulus factor" – that is essential to sparking motivation – is much more complex and requires tapping into the hidden and often unexplored depths of the human psyche and drawing upon the swirling mass of suppressed emotions, forgotten memories, unarticulated beliefs and values each one of us possesses as a human being. It is any one of these which could be stimulated (from within or from outside the psyche) to trigger a specific set of behaviors which lead to enhanced performance.

## The research for this book

Motivation therefore has to be stimulated. In my research for this book about 1000 people across four continents were asked the question: "What really motivates you?" From the vast number of responses a pattern began to emerge, relating to 17 different clusters of stimuli that would ignite a person's motivation.

The research also revealed that the large majority of people say they are self-motivated. Since the conventional view is that a key role for a manager is to motivate people, it begs the question whether managers can actually do so if their people are self-motivated.

The overall conclusion that I came to – perhaps a controversial one – is that all motivation is self-motivation. There is no other type of motivation.

# 2

# The nature of a stimulus

A stimulus is a minute parcel of energy that triggers the expenditure of a much larger amount of energy. To release motivational energies requires such a stimulus.

It is often the smallest of inflexions of the conductor's baton that creates the difference in producing a great performance from an orchestra. Or it might be the raising of the conductor's eyebrow that will stimulate every player to lift their whole soul on to a musical phrase. Furthermore it can be the audience that stimulates the conductor to stimulate an even greater performance from the orchestra. Whilst a conductor will have his back to the audience the quality of the silence is critically important in providing a stimulus to the conductor.
*Howard Shelley, pianist and conductor*

## The stimulus requirement

To initiate any movement requires a stimulus. Your car might have a powerful engine and a tank full of fuel, but it will not move without the stimulus of a spark when you turn the ignition key. A nudge of the steering wheel or a slight pressure on the accelerator pedal or brake will provide a further stimulus to direct the movement of the car.

For a person to move also requires a stimulus. You might have a lot of energy, a strong heart and powerful mind, but you will not move in any given direction unless you receive a stimulus to initiate that movement. The same principle applies to any organization. A company will not move in any given direction unless there is a specific stimulus that energizes its people.

A stimulus is a very small parcel of energy that triggers the expenditure of a much larger amount of energy. It is like a spark or a catalyst. A stimulus initiates movement. Thus the recommendation of a friend to try out a new restaurant will provide the stimulus to visit such a restaurant. At work a series of complaints from customers about delivery delays might provide the stimulus for a major review of distribution procedures and subsequent improvements.

In most walks of life – and also at work – the impact of a stimulus or stimuli is neglected. We tend to concentrate our attention on how the energy is expended rather than on what initiates it. Thus in business we focus our attention on such big topics as productivity, staffing levels, salaries and logistics (which all relate to how energy is used) but often neglect to consider the essential triggers that motivate people.

All our decisions, all our actions, all our behaviors and all our communications are the result of the stimuli we receive and the movements they initiate. If we just take body language, for example, every expression on our face and every movement of our fingers, hands, arms and legs is in response to a set of stimuli we have received, either

> All communications can be traced to a specified stimulus or set of stimuli and the same applies to all our behaviors

externally or internally. We cross our arms when listening to another person, because we are subconsciously resisting what the other person is saying. Whatever that statement is, it is a stimulus that prompts the movement of crossing our arms and puts us into defensive mode. All communications can be traced to a specified stimulus or set of stimuli and the same applies to all our behaviors.

To understand people, therefore, it is not only necessary to understand their behavior but also to understand what stimulates such behavior. For example, one person interviewed for this book, Jonathan McMillan, Clinical Project Manager with Schering-Plough, says: "I wear a bow-tie because it sends a signal 'I'm not like everyone else.' It says: 'I'm an individual.' Most people wear conventional ties. I wear a 'bow-tie'. It says I don't conform completely."

The bow-tie Jonathan McMillan wears is a stimulus alerting people to the fact there is something different about him. In this case the stimulus is conscious and therefore intended, but in many cases it is subconscious and unintended. To understand the impact we have on other people we therefore have to raise from our subconscious the various stimuli that we emit and consciously consider their impact on other people.

## The two types of responses to stimuli

There can be two types of responses to any given stimulus:

- an automatic response
- a more complex, considered response.

With an automatic response there is no option on how to respond to a stimulus, whilst in the second case there is a range of options to be considered on how to do so.

In the first case the response is normally pre-programmed and no thinking is required. There is a reflex reaction to the stimulus. When we act without thinking, or develop habits or get into routines, we are effectively putting ourselves into automatic mode in response to any given stimulus. We put ourselves on autopilot. Such responses are subconscious.

A mechanical example of an automatic response to a stimulus is the use of a thermostat in conjunction with a heating device. When the heating device is on, the temperature of the room increases. This causes a small piece of metal in the thermostat to expand. When a certain temperature is reached, the expanding metal releases a switch and thus turns off the heating device. The increase of room temperature becomes the stimulus to reduce room temperature, and vice versa. The response is automatic. As the room temperature lowers, the piece of metal in the thermostat contracts, thus allowing the switch to reconnect and turn on the heating device again. The reconnection is thus a second stimulus that activates the heater.

As human beings we also allow ourselves to respond automatically to specific stimuli. Every time we detect, interpret and react to a new stimulus we condition ourselves to react the same way the next time we receive this specific stimulus. This gradual conditioning leads us to behave in automatic "nonconscious" mode. Tor Nørretranders (1998) argues that most of our behavior is nonconscious: "People mainly function nonconsciously ... we are not consciously aware of all the information our mind processes or of the causes of all the behaviors we produce, or of the origin of all the feelings we experience."

Most forms of training are based on the premise that repeated conscious practice will eventually lead to subconscious practice. Through ongoing learning we put ourselves on "autopilot" and develop habits that save us energy and thinking time. Who thinks about each note being played on a piano? Who thinks about each word we utter? The answer is only students. If we want to improve our approach to motivation we have to study our own behavior and the way it acts as a stimulus in relation to other people.

We could not perform effectively if we had to think empirically every morning how to tie up a shoelace or how to drive a car or which route we should use to go to work. The original stimuli, whilst necessary for the initial learning, effectively become redundant when the response has to be repeated time and time. We subsequently ignore these original stimuli in our quest for efficiency. We no longer need to look at a shoelace when we tie it up, nor do we any longer need to refer to the stimulus of a street sign on the way to work.

However, as these original stimuli become redundant and we increasingly perform on autopilot, we risk a slow deterioration in performance. We neglect to see that the shoelace is worn and might break at an unpropitious moment; we neglect to see a new speed limit on the way to work.

When we continue for any long period on autopilot we tend to become complacent, unthinking and uncreative. We begin to take everything for granted and fail to detect danger signals, blocking out vital stimuli that should spark positive changes in behavior. Our minds close in and we resist change, seeing it as threatening the comfort zones that have become the by-product of our ease of routine and habit. Our

> The key to success is strike a careful balance between the vital automatic responses needed to survive and the use of more complex, considered responses

minds along with our hearts and souls become flabby. In opting for the energy-saving "autopilot" routine we gradually become unaware of essential new stimuli and thus fail to respond accordingly. This happens frequently in business when managers ignore such new stimuli as looming competitive threats or deterioration in employee morale or an increasing volume of negative customer feedback. By putting ourselves on autopilot and failing to respond to new stimuli we become uncompetitive and risk going out of business. The key to success is strike a careful balance between the vital automatic responses needed to survive and the use of the more complex, considered responses.

Out of necessity all human beings are programmed with automatic responses or reflex reactions. Some of them are pre-programmed into our genes and effectively form the hard-wiring of the neurological systems that are assigned to us prior to birth. One of the first tests doctors give to newborn babies is to snap their fingers in front of their eyes and see if they blink. If they do, then they have normal reflex reactions. Later on in life, during medical examinations, you will find doctors tapping your knee with a hammer to see if your foot kicks up as a reflex reaction. The snapping of fingers and the tapping of knees are stimuli which effect a reflex reaction.

However, in addition to these hard-wired reflex programs, we also possess subconscious "learnt software." As a result of our various experiences throughout life we continually accumulate an increasing range of further reflex reactions by subconsciously loading software into our personal control systems. Rather than have to think through our response to every situation we face in life or at work, we learn from our experiences and convert this learning into prepared responses that save us the effort of having to think about it next time this situation occurs. Regrettably, such learning is often highly imperfect and our automatic responses cause innumerable problems. This happens when people "fly off the handle," or "act without thinking," or exhibit impulsive behavior. Road rage is one such example. Another example is avoidance behavior. We make excuses when asked to do something we don't want, or we look the other way when someone we don't like passes by.

Our personal control systems and related software reside not just in our brains but in a complex electro-chemical neurological network that stretches to our hearts, stomachs and mysteriously (because no scientist can yet explain this) to our souls and spirits as well.

When there is an automatic (reflex) reaction, we are subconsciously reacting to a conscious stimulus. A fast-working subconscious process takes over from the more limited and slower working conscious process that we use when we think about something. Survival responses necessitate this, thus when a horse careers towards us there is no time to think, we just leap out of the way. When there is a conscious intervention the process of responding to a stimulus is slowed down dramatically. Reflex reactions are exceptionally fast, whilst responses that we consciously consider tend to be very slow. The brain is a very cumbersome and slow-working instrument. Furthermore, it tends to operate in a very negative "can't do" way. ("I can't do this because it will make me feel bad.") The brain is very good at finding problems and has been programmed over time immemorial to do so. However, it is very poor at creating solutions. These tend to originate in the heart and the soul. A "brainwave" is actually the conscious detection of an idea that *we ourselves* create from the center of our "selves" as human beings. That center is our heart and soul, not our brain. The idea emerges from our subconscious "self" and stimulates our consciousness.

To manage stimuli more effectively, and our responses to them, we thus need to be clear whether or not we are acting in automatic mode or whether we can consciously intercede to create a more considered and effective response. Regrettably our brains, being so negative, tend to deceive us and often we rationalize our automatic behavior as considered behavior. In this way we explain away our actions with rationales invented after the event. We are all full of excuses and frequently fail to reveal the real reasons. As Eduardo Gianetti (2000) says: "We tend to think in our own favor and are loathe to think against ourselves. That is why 90 per cent of American drivers think they are above average."

To become more effective we need to re-examine and possibly change the software that we have created to respond to different types of stimuli, as well as re-examine and possibly change the types of stimuli we respond to. This is far from easy, as we would be asking ourselves (and others) to change the habits of a lifetime, as well as change a wide variety of deep-rooted mannerisms, traits, beliefs and values.

The two different types of responses to stimuli can be represented diagrammatically, as in Figs 2.1 and 2.2.

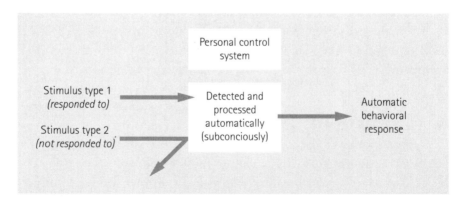

### Fig 2.1

Automatic response

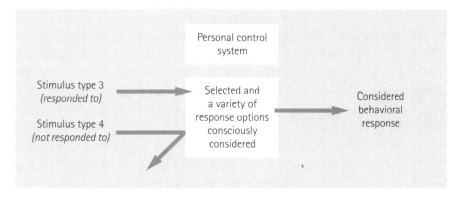

**Fig 2.2**

Complex considered response

# Stimulus-detection mechanisms

In both types of response we use a number of mechanisms to detect and select stimuli we subconsciously or consciously respond to. These mechanisms are our senses and include not only the five traditional sensing devices (eyes, ears, nose, tongue, skin), which are physical, but also an additional psychological sensing device.

The psychological sensing device involves our emotions and how we feel about a selected stimulus. Psychologically we will sense whether a person is "warm" or "cold" towards us, and feel good or bad as a result. Our emotions arise from these feelings and provide a stimulus to our behavior. Thus when our boss shouts at us we feel bad. There might be an automatic response in that we go quiet and avoid his or her gaze. There might also be a considered response in that we review our options on how best to react in the circumstances. Emotions therefore have a critical role to play in the way we respond to stimuli.

> Emotions have a critical role to play in the way we respond to stimuli

Closely related to our emotions and how we feel is our value and belief system and what we stand for (or don't stand for) in life. The home of our value and belief system is our soul from which our spirit emanates. When our belief system is attacked by a negative stimulus (for example, abuse from our boss) then the spirit in which we respond becomes critical. Some people allow themselves to become dispirited as a result of negative stimuli, whilst others will react in a positive spirit.

In other words our hearts and souls as well as our minds have a critical bearing on our responses to selected stimuli, especially the behavior of other people. Not only is the way we select stimuli important, but to get the stimulus factor to work for us we have to develop a deep awareness of our feelings and emotions, as well as of the deep-rooted spirits that drive us forward in response to a selected stimulus. By creating this awareness we are then in a positive position to effect change and improvement, should we desire it. This is critically important when it comes to "relationship-oriented" jobs, for example in the area of customer service.

## The stimulus factor and change

To change behavior requires a change of stimulus.

People often repeat the same stimuli without being aware they are having no impact at all in eliciting the desired response. For example, many of us are prone to repeating the same old arguments over and over again without ever effecting the changes we are arguing for. Often we achieve the reverse of that intended: we alienate people by going on and on about something. People soon tire of us repeating ourselves incessantly. Children often exhibit such annoying behaviors. They fail to realize that the repeated use of a given stimulus, for example "I want to watch this program on television," fails to elicit the desired response from their parents. In fact the stimulus invokes a movement away from what the child desires. The repeated demand stimulates an angry response from the parent, who begins to shout at the child. This in turn stimulates a further, "But mum, you don't understand…" response from the child.

In other words the stimuli used have not been effective. When a desired response has not been obtained it is often necessary to change the stimulus rather than repeat it, as is our tendency.

The failure of a stimulus to be effective in achieving the desired response often happens at work too. An edict from head office exhorts people to cut costs by cutting back on travel, training, overtime and virtually everything which can cut back on. The edict is a stimulus aimed at motivating people to move in the direction of cutting costs. Frequently the result of the stimulus is demotivation and whilst people cut back on direct costs (such as travel) they actually perform less effectively and increase the indirect costs by producing less. What happens is one step forward and two back – a result of an inappropriate ill-thought-through stimulus.

A key factor in the art of management therefore is the way we manage the wide range of stimuli needed to motivate people to perform effectively, as well as motivate customers to buy from us. We need to be constantly changing the stimuli.

We not only have to change the stimuli we use to motivate other people but also those we use to motivate ourselves. Thus the first time we hear a recording of Pavarotti sing "Nessun dorma" it is probable that the hairs on our necks will stand on end and tingle. However, should we put the track on repeat play and listen to it continuously for three hours we will find that something different happens. The tingle effect wears off pretty quickly. Repeated application of the same stimuli has decreasing efficacy. To motivate others as well as ourselves, fresh stimuli must be used frequently.

> To effect change requires a change of stimuli

In other words a stimulus has only a short-term impact in unleashing motivational energy. A once-off use of a specific stimulus, or even a repeated use of it, will lead to gradual motivational loss as the effect of the stimulus wears off. This is the "stimulus effect" (or "stimulus curve") and is illustrated in Fig. 2.3.

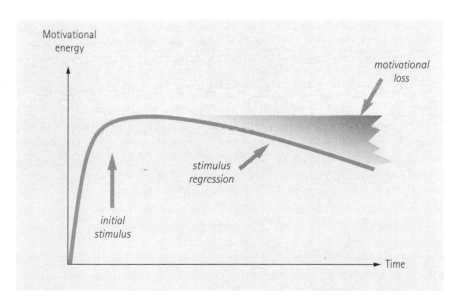

**Fig 2.3**

The stimulus effect

## The stimulus factor and incentives

It is for this reason that pay or financial incentives have such a limited impact on performance. In all probability the incentive (the carrot) will work the first time you offer it to people. However, its effect will wear off as time passes by. Repeated use of the same pay incentives will also have diminishing returns. To be effective in sustaining levels of motivation fresh stimuli must be used from time to time, as indicated in Fig. 2.4.

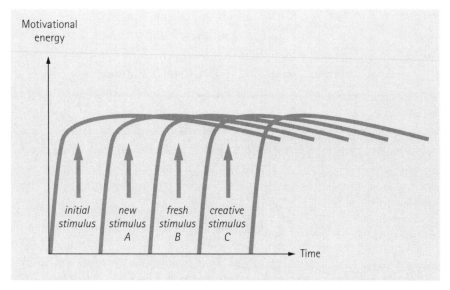

**Fig 2.4**

The stimulus effect: adding fresh stimuli

Both Figures 2.3 and 2.4, depicting the "stimulus effect" (or "stimulus curve"), are applicable to all aspects of the management and motivation process.

Stimulation is a basic human need that adds an essential third dimension to each of the needs specified in the well-known motivation hierarchy. We require a stimulus for everything we do whether it be eating, drinking, socializing, loving, working or achieving success (however we define it).

# Stimulus deprivation

A life without stimulation would be like being confined to a dark sound-proofed room for the rest of your life and being denied any human contact. You would be fed through mechanical devices with vitamin tablets, mineral supplements, tasteless carbohydrate stodge, pure protein and plain water. It might be nutritionally correct but otherwise it would be dreadful. The tour-guide at Alcatraz (near San Francisco) has such a story. A wonderful meal used to be served up to prisoners in solitary confinement, but before they could eat it the three courses (soup; steak, chips, carrots; ice-cream and chocolate sauce) were tipped into a blender and rendered into a smooth tasteless goo which was then handed to them on a plate. All the nutrients were there but something else wasn't.

Even so, when we are deprived of physical stimuli (such as light, sound and human contact) we can still fall back on the power of internal stimuli. The stories of the hostages in the Lebanon showed how they preserved their sanity by drawing upon the deepest and innermost reaches of their souls to stimulate their thought processes and create hopes that in turn further stimulated them to persist in keeping their sanity intact and surviving. Our souls and spirits potentially have immense powers and can survive when everything else seems to be failing.

To quote Brian Keenan (1992) from his book *An Evil Cradling* about his time as a hostage in the Lebanon:

The prison was, after the first few weeks, a place where there were no incidents to stimulate the mind or the imagination; there was no color, no character, nothing on which the mind and the personality might feed and nurture itself into meaning.

Later, after John McCarthy had been placed in the cell with him, he writes:

As the days of absolute darkness continued we thought that we could not endure much more. Yet something in the human spirit seeks a way to overcome such oppression. ... We needed the stimulus of another person, his sympathy, his critical judgement to help guide us. We need his assurance that the world was worth the effort.

Nelson Mandela's 26 years in the Robben Island prison is another example of the power of internal stimulation in the "long walk to freedom" (1994).

With each week resembling the one before, one must make an effort to recall what day and month it is. One of the first things I did was to make a calendar on the wall of my cell. Losing a sense of time is an easy way to lose one's grip and one's sanity.

When suffering immense deprivation the process of creating a calendar and the process of it ticking it off become a stimulus. It stimulates the soul and helps retain a person's sanity. Later Mandela writes:

As a prisoner I was entitled to write and receive only one letter every six months. Sometimes six months would go by without a letter. To be allowed one letter in six months and then not to receive it is a great blow. When letters did arrive, they were cherished. A letter was like the summer rain that could make even the desert bloom.

A single letter in six months becomes a revitalizing stimulus. Again it stimulates the soul and re-energizes a person.

Most of us are not aware of our needs for stimuli, the dangers of stimulus deprivation and the suffering caused by it. Yet we are all prone to mild forms of this affliction. When we have nothing to do or have to carry out prolonged repetitive tasks we risk becoming bored and thus less effective in what we do.

In a management situation the challenge is to create sufficient stimuli to prevent this happening. Too often we hear stories of people becoming "stale" or requiring "new challenges."

## Stimulus saturation

The reason we travel, dine out at new restaurants, listen to new music, take exercise and even change jobs is because of our essential ongoing require-ments for stimulation. Yet we can have too much of a good thing.

The reverse of stimulus deprivation is stimulus saturation. Often we just have too much stimulation to cope with. We become saturated with it and then perversely find ourselves lacking in stimulation. We come bored with too much flickering television, too many sickening nights out, too many microwaving restaurants.

When we have become saturated with stimuli we suddenly find it difficult to sustain concentration and focus on any one task. We are so used to being stimulated that a momentary lapse in stimulation creates a negative reaction. We cannot sit still and we have this desperate urge to do something. Yet paradoxically when we are saturated with stimulation the more we seek the less it seems to satisfy us. Our attention spans becomes shorter and shorter and we begin to suffer from an adult form of ADD (Attention Deficit Disorder).

Stimulus saturation is increasingly a problem in the work situation. The constant flow of e-mail messages, mobile phone calls, interrupts to meetings and the need to be moving all the time are symptoms of this affliction. Executives now demand one-page reports and one-minute presentations – they don't have time for more. Everything has to be at a fast pace. Presidents have diary secretaries who schedule their time down to the last minute.

> The speed of the modern workplace means that we deprive ourselves of the essential stimulation of social contact and soul-searching

Instant communications are the order of the day, together with a fast food diet of sound-bites and slogans. Company strategies are reduced to half-page mission statements and six core values.

The speed of the modern workplace means that we hardly have time for each other and that we deprive ourselves of the essential stimulation of social contact and soul-searching. When we are saturated with external stimuli we become less wise by the hour. Perversely, when we are deprived of such stimuli we have the opportunity to harness our internal stimuli to enhance the essential wisdom of how we should live and work.

## Stimulus balance

The challenge for each one of us – and also for any manager – is to strike an appropriate balance between too much and too little stimulation in our lives and work. It is a precarious balance and can be easily tipped one way or the other, with a resultant negative impact on motivation and performance.

Success in life – and high performance in particular – are critically dependent on the creation and application of a balanced set of stimuli, together with an effective response to them. In business management this becomes an art form. Not only does a business manager have to identify and produce the appropriate stimuli to secure a response from a customer or an employee, but they also have to obtain the right balance. Too little or too much can be counter-productive.

## Negative and positive stimuli

Stimuli can be either positive or negative. Positive stimuli can make us feel good, whilst negative stimuli have the potential to make us feel bad. The two are totally interdependent. It is impossible to feel good without having felt bad (and vice versa). The reason paradise will never exist is that if we ever reach it we won't know we're there because we will have had no experience of feeling bad. Our lives are a series of comparative, not absolute experiences. Without failure we cannot experience success, without rejection we cannot experience acceptance, without hate we cannot experience love.

> To move forward we need to experience both negative and positive stimuli

Thus to move forward we need to experience both negative and positive stimuli. The danger of positive thinking is that we attempt to eliminate the necessary negative stimuli in our lives. Fear has its place and so has pain. The art is to manage such negative stimuli wisely rather than destructively. Awareness of a competitive threat is such an example. Wise managers respond positively and creatively, whilst the less wise destroy their organizations by denying the threat. As Peter Senge (1990) wrote in his book *The Fifth Discipline*:

In most companies that fail, there is abundant evidence in advance that the firm is in trouble. The evidence goes unheeded, however, even when individual managers are aware of it. The organization as a whole cannot recognize impending threats, understand the implications of those threats, or come up with alternatives.

To get the stimulus factor to work effectively for us we have to be brutally honest about what makes us feel good and what makes us feel bad in the jobs we do. We have to accept the need for negative stimuli in order to generate and apply the appropriate positive stimuli. Equally important, we have to discover what our customers and employees feel about us, whether it is good or really bad. The expression of such feelings is vital to the way we stimulate improvements to our businesses and the way we manage and motivate people.

# The stimulus transfer and chain reactions

In many cases the response to a stimulus becomes the stimulus itself. A domino effect takes place, in which the energy released from the initial stimulus provides a second stimulus, which in turn leads to a third stimulus.

The chain reaction of energy release that occurs when an initial stimulus sparks a series of stimuli is unpredictable. It is seen, for example, when a flock of birds swirls around in the air. A minor deviation in direction by one bird will stimulate a whole series of directional changes by the other birds. It is also seen in epidemics when the initial person infected with a virus stimulates a rash of the disease across a large population of people. Malcolm Gladwell (2000) explains that "little things can make a big difference" and provides many examples of how one small incident can create major changes. He asserts that: "Ideas and products and messages and behaviors spread just like viruses do." One virus stimulates a reaction in a person. The stimulus (the virus) is then transferred to other people and creates a chain reaction – causing an epidemic.

This concept of stimulus transfer is vitally important in attempting to understand organization change – and why so many change programs fail.

Mass hysteria is another sign of stimulus transfer, as is the popular notion of "following the sheep." Often the stimulus comes in the form of "auto-suggestion" whereby an individual is unaware that their behavior is in response to a certain stimulus. Furthermore, they are unaware that their own behavioral response to a stimulus creates stimulus transfer and similar responses amongst others. When one person claps everyone else claps. When one person yawns everyone else begins to yawn. As soon as one person stands up to leave the room the rest follow. All these are examples of stimulus transfer.

Stimulus transfer can have both positive and negative consequences. In trying to effect organization change it is critical to create positive stimuli (transmitted by positive carriers) to oppose the negative stimuli created by "the bad apples in the pack." Within organizations stimulus transfer is often a battle between the antibodies and pathogens, between the carriers/transmitters of the positive messages and the carriers/transmitters of the negative messages.

# The stimulus factor and motivation

One of the key conclusions from the research for this book is that motivation is inextricably linked to the way we respond to a wide variety of internal and external stimuli. The number of stimuli that we encounter every day is vast, yet we respond to very few. That response is a product of our motivational drives. The research revealed that these motivational responses can be linked to one or more of 17 different clusters of stimuli. These are outlined in the next chapter.

# 3

# The clusters of motivational stimuli

A pattern emerged from more than 1000 responses that were
given to the question "What really motivates you?" This showed
that there are 17 broad clusters of stimuli which can have an
impact on people's motivation.

## What really motivates people?

What really motivates people and why is that many people we meet seem
demotivated? Why is that in many organizations I visit the staff look
miserable and complain of low morale, whilst in others the people "buzz"
and appear to be highly motivated?

My research for this book sought to answers these questions by asking
approximately 1000 people: "What really motivates you?" Interviewees
included people working in call centers, bank employees, government staff,
taxi drivers, construction workers and unemployed students. They also
included Sir Richard Branson of the Virgin Group; Sir Michael Bichard, a
top civil servant; Howard Shelley, the international concert pianist and
conductor; and Bob Dickinson, President of Carnival Cruises in the USA.
The interviews were conducted across four continents from America to
Europe, the Far East and Africa.

# Emerging patterns: the stimulus clusters

From the responses that were provided it became increasingly clear that when people talked about "what motivated them" they were not talking about a "permanent state of being" but of specific events and situations that led them to "feeling motivated" (or "demotivated"). These events were effectively stimuli that triggered a release of positive energies from within. It is these positive energies, together with the way they are directed towards desired outcomes, that constitutes motivation. In fact all motivation is initiated by a stimulus. Each stimulus is temporary – and so is the level of motivation that results. To sustain motivation therefore requires a constant supply of stimuli, whether they be internal or external. The research revealed that most people experience a wide variety of different motivations (or demotivations) which are stimulated by a wide variety of internal and external factors.

> To sustain motivation requires a constant supply of stimuli, whether they be internal or external

The next chapter explores in depth the subject of motivation, whilst this one presents the 17 broad clusters of motivational stimuli that emerged from the pattern of responses.

First are extracts of six sample responses from the large numbers of people interviewed, together with a few illustrations of how specific statements were linked to one of the clusters of motivational stimuli. The list of 17 clusters then follows.

## Sir Michael Bichard

Permanent Secretary, Department of Education and Employment, UK

*What really motivates you?*

Increasingly as I get older what motivates me is making a difference in the real world. My motivation is internal. It is the fear of failure. It is needing to make the best of my potential. I will always deliver. My internal motivation will carry me through the most hostile terrain.

| *Motivational stimulus* | *Cluster* |
| --- | --- |
| Making a difference | Aspirational |
| Fear of failure | Emotional |
| Carry me through the most hostile terrain | Negative |

## Claire Brand, General Manager

Hallmark Business Expressions, USA

### *What really motivates you?*

In terms of what motivates me, it's the ability to see where I can make a difference and then do it ... whether it's business results or raising a family. Learning and being challenged to go to the next level is very motivating. Challenging yourself to stay at the cutting edge in your profession is motivating. Working with bright individuals who make you think differently or add to your thinking to make it better is motivating. Seeing others succeed that you have worked with or mentored is motivating.

| *Motivational stimulus* | *Cluster* |
|---|---|
| Making a difference, being challenged | Aspirational |
| Learning to go to the next level | Learning |
| Working with bright individuals | Social + inspirational |
| Seeing others succeed | Altruistic |

## Sanchia Gallifent

Sales Supervisor, British Airways Travel Shops, Windsor, UK

### *What really motivates you?*

My need in life is to be liked and loved. I'm a very emotional person and I get hurt very easily. I have a need to be needed and to be loved and liked. What motivates me is people. Why I get up in the morning and go to work is that I want to find out what people want and then exceed their expectations. What motivates me is that I can talk to people, understand what they want and what their expectations are. It drives me all the time – not just at work, but everything I do.

| *Motivational stimulus* | *Cluster* |
|---|---|
| To be liked and loved | Personal value |
| I get hurt easily | Emotional + negative |
| Exceed expectations | Aspirational + altruistic |
| What motivates me is people | Social |

## Brian Longstreet

Director, Gastroenterology/CNS Business Unit, Schering-Plough, USA

### *What really motivates you?*

What motivates me is being challenged from an intellectual standpoint. It is breaking new ground and doing things people have not done before. It is a sense of accomplishment – when it works and it is successful. An example is that we built from the ground upwards a new unit on disease management. It was a different way of working with our customers. It provided a program as opposed to products. Money doesn't motivate me. I'm doing as much as I can.

| Motivational stimulus | Cluster |
| --- | --- |
| Being challenged | Aspirational |
| Breaking new ground | Discovery |
| Sense of accomplishment | Personal value |

## Lisa O'Brien, Secretary

WPA Health Insurance, UK

*What really motivates you?*

WPA! It is a special company – the team and the people. Everyone mucks in. The quality of everything here is high. It's nice place to work. The bosses are tough but fair. They expect the best. Julian Stainton [Chief Executive] is inspirational. He creates a buzz, excitement, energy and enthusiasm. Surroundings influence people. Everyone dresses smartly. Everyone is positive and happy. You can't be grumpy here and get away with it.

| Motivational stimulus | Cluster |
| --- | --- |
| The team and the people | Social |
| Nice place to work. Surroundings influence people | Environmental |
| He creates a buzz, excitement... | Inspirational |

## Tanya Pillay-Nair

Front Office Manager, Grand Hyatt Hotel, Singapore

*What really motivates you?*

What motivates me is a sense of achievement, a sense of making a difference. The environment I work in also has an impact on my motivation. It has to be positive with a lot of camaraderie and humor. It needs to be a place where I want to come into work in the morning. Suitable remuneration is important. I don't want to feel I'm being taken advantage of. The ability to change things motivates me – without having to go through too much hierarchy, protocol and bureaucracy. I need to have the knowledge that I can effect positive change.

| Motivational stimulus | Cluster |
| --- | --- |
| Sense of achievement, making a difference | Aspirational |
| Environment has an impact | Environmental |
| Camaraderie and humor | Social + diversionary |
| Suitable remuneration is important | Reward (financial) |
| Ability to change things | Freedom |

Even though these extracts are but a very small sample of the 1000 responses that were collected, a pattern gradually emerged as the research exercise proceeded. This pattern separated into broad clusters of motivational stimuli. A list of these 17 clusters follows, together with some examples of the responses that were grouped under each cluster. Some of the stimuli that trigger motivation can be drawn from more than one cluster. Thus camaraderie is definitely a social stimulus, whilst humor is a diversionary one. The same would apply to "exceeding the expectations of customers." The stimulus here is both aspirational and altruistic.

# The 17 clusters of motivational stimuli

## 1 Aspirational stimuli

*Hopes, dreams, challenges, vision, goals, mission, achievement, success, winning, etc.*

What really motivates me is:
- wanting to succeed;
- a great challenge;
- having targets – if three days go by and I'm not hitting my target of 50, I say to myself "I've got to get it!";
- having something to aim towards – people like to discover their own goals;
- taking on things that are intuitively difficult and then succeeding;
- making a difference to a large company like this;
- on Friday I set myself a lot of tasks and accomplished all these;
- when I clear all my work for the day;
- exceeding expectations, including my own expectations;
- satisfying my customers and knowing it;
- the fact we got to number one last year;
- seeing everyone be successful.

## 2 Learning stimuli

*Self-improvement, personal development, knowledge etc.*

What really motivates me is:
- learning through good and bad;
- a thirst for knowledge about what I'm doing;

- realizing that failure is not the end of the world but a learning opportunity;
- when I do a really great training class with employees – it gives me a buzz: I learn from them and they learn from me;
- learning from others: for example, I learnt something from my five-year-old daughter recently – about surprising people with rewards;
- a good day when I have learnt something and grown.

## 3 Discovery stimuli

*Revelation, curiosity, questioning etc.*

What really motivates me is:

- finding out what's going here – we communicate a lot, we walk the floor;
- that our boss is always asking us what we think;
- getting to know the real person and discovering what's important to them in their day;
- that there is always an element of the unknown about every day – that excites me;
- I love my job, I'm paid to be inquisitive;
- that we put a lot of emphasis here on finding better ways of doing things.

## 4 Diversionary stimuli

*Fun, entertainment, games, sport, distraction etc.*

What really motivates me is:

- that we have lots of quizzes and games here;
- that we have lots of fun days;
- when I get to take my team out – we had a three-hour lunch on a boat recently;
- making my customers' and teams' lives a little more enjoyable – we have a lot of fun;
- that we can be in a very serious meeting, for example about cost reduction, and we still have a good laugh;
- we find any excuse here to celebrate things – we have a great time.

## 5 Reward stimuli – financial and related

*Incentives, prizes, awards, pay, bonuses, etc.*

What really motivates me is:

- money, I'll be honest about it;
- that I work hard and the bonus comes;

- that we get gift vouchers when we put in extra effort, for example clearing backlogs;
- the financial rewards – it's not the only thing but I think it's important;
- is a competitive desire and getting the financial results;
- money and the success it brings with it – a bad day is when I don't take much money.

# 6 Personal value stimuli

*Appreciation, recognition, being valued, etc.*

What really motivates me is:

- that last Friday I left my old department; everyone signed a card – the comments were fantastic; I was moved;
- being valued as an individual;
- I want to be unique and valued – when I receive a call from a headhunter I find it motivating;
- I was delighted to have a salary increase recently but the words my boss used in telling me why I'd got the increase meant much more;
- when my suggestions are accepted and I feel I'm doing something valuable;
- when someone massages my ego, for example saying to me "you would really be good at this."

# 7 Inspirational stimuli

*Art, music, writing, creativity, "eureka" moments, brainwaves etc.*

What really motivates me is:

- the inspiration I get from my boss to come up with new ideas;
- being creative. I enjoy being involved in improving things, in changes – it gets my pulse racing;
- when innovation turns real – that's when I get my juice;
- finding creative solutions to problems;
- creating value – I do this on a daily basis, finding unique ways of letting everyone in the team know how valuable they are;
- hinking of ideas for doing something good.

## 8 Altruistic stimuli

*Care, giving, doing good, philanthropy etc.*

What really motivates me is:

- helping customers – if you achieve something for them you know they'll come back;
- simply giving people time;
- that everyone in our team wants to help each other;
- getting up in the morning, finding what my customers want and then exceeding their expectations;
- that we run our business on added value – it's not just profit, we like to give more than our customers bargain for;
- that I have 2500 people in my team and I get a buzz when they're happy – it's electrifying when it happens.

## 9 Social stimuli

*Family, love, community, team, being with people, communicating etc.*

What really motivates me is:

- my family: I care about them; I want them to be proud of me;
- we have lots of social events here, for example trips to Brussels and Paris;
- working together as a team – we get a real buzz, we thrive on teamwork;
- that I work with a good crowd here;
- that we spend a lot of time communicating with each other;
- getting a buzz from meeting people.

## 10 Basic stimuli

*Survival, health, food, sex, activity etc.*

What really motivates me is:

- doing yoga – it helps me attain peak performance for my work;
- that every day around 3.00 pm we stop the show (the office) and do a little exercise, approximately 15 minutes callisthenics – the team love it;
- doing things – I am a doer, I like activity;
- action – I can't sit still for too long;
- activity – I need to be active, I couldn't have an office job;
- keeping in a job;
- just being able to support my family;

- security – I don't like risks;
- keeping healthy. I lost my mother at 50; I pinch myself in the morning and tell myself "I'm still alive": that motivates me.

## 11 Emotional stimuli

*Feelings, passions, drives, desires etc.*

What really motivates me is:

- that the emotions I had as a child make we want to understand people better;
- fear of failure;
- when my customers hug me: yesterday when I opened up at 9.00 am there were a couple of customers waiting for me who I hadn't seen for a while – they almost picked me and hugged me;
- enjoying what I'm doing;
- feeling special when I make other people feel special;
- that I just love my job;
- working in a bookstore – I just love books.

## 12 Demand stimuli

*Orders, instructions, commands, threats, requests etc.*

What really motivates me is:

- doing what my boss wants and pleasing him;
- when the company president asks me to do something and I do it well;
- having a manager who gives clear directions;
- having a boss who is tough and fair, and who expects the best;
- I have a lot of respect for my boss and I'm happy to do what he tells me;

## 13 Environmental stimuli

*Décor, furniture, light, sound, space, atmosphere, climate etc.*

What really motivates me is:

- the environment here – it's comfortable and safe;
- having a good working atmosphere around you;
- the high standards we have in everything here – the toilets are spotless, we have a first-class canteen and overall an excellent environment;
- the countryside – there's a lot of driving in my job and I just love the countryside I pass through;

- that when you walk in here there's a presence: you feel it in everything around you – you walk in the locker room and there's a presence, you just feel it, it's the energy in the surroundings;
- everyone dresses smartly here – the surroundings influence people.

## 14 Freedom stimuli

*Choice, risk, personal decision making.*

What really motivates me is:

- that as long as you do your job properly here you get no bother;
- that the hit-rate I get from cold-calling is totally down to me;
- being left to get on with things;
- being trusted to do what I believe is necessary for our customers;
- the total freedom I have in my job – effectively I am my own boss: I even choose the hours I work;
- all the opportunities I get to make a difference.

## 15 Negative stimuli

*Setback, failure, criticism, problems.*

What really motivates me is:

- helping people out of a crisis; unfortunately for many people it takes a crisis to motivate them to change;
- picking myself up after I've been knocked down – I was taught that as a child;
- learning from mistakes;
- failure – you can't be successful without experiencing failure; I'm too embarrassed to tell you all my failures;
- remembering what happened to me 15 years ago: I was fired – it was the best thing that ever happened to me;
- once I had a boss who was a bastard, he was a bully – I just decided to stand up to him; now I always stand up to people.

## 16 Change stimuli

*Out of routine, new job, travel, new challenge, new people.*

What really motivates me is:

- variety – no two cases I deal with are the same;
- that each day is different – different customers, different challenges;
- improving things, making changes; I find repetition frustrating – I wouldn't be comfortable doing the same task over and over again, overfamiliarity brings boredom;

- newness, I find it exciting – new work, new people, new places;
- opportunities to move around – I've moved eight times in this company;
- travel – I couldn't be in the same place all the time; I'd hate it if it was the same office every day of the working year.

## 17 Spiritual stimuli

*Understanding and expression of self, principles, beliefs, values etc.*

What really motivates me is:

- my value system and my life's dream – to do good for others;
- discovering a meaning to my life and my life's purpose;
- belief – senior leaders must have their ideals, but sticking to principles is tough; if leaders take short-cuts on the principles they espouse then they lose credibility;
- doing what I believe is right: if my company president says "do it" I will only do it if I believe it's right; if I believe it's wrong I won't do it;
- trying to put into practice all my principles;
- doing everything from the heart – I try to be genuine and sincere in whatever I do or say.

# Three groupings of clusters

Because of the subjective nature of the responses and the lack of any available objective measure (this was deliberate), I am reluctant to assign "weight," "importance" or "priority" to any given cluster of motivational stimuli. I have therefore not prepared the above list in order of "weight," because even though certain "weightings" can be deduced I am not convinced that they are meaningful.

Despite this, the number of responses assigned to each cluster did vary and did reveal a very loose weighting of predominant, middling and weak stimuli. Whilst three loose weightings might be far from meaningful, for the purpose of debate they are presented in Table 3.1. However, I would stress that not too much attention should be paid to these groupings. I suspect that the stimuli present in the weak group are those to which people give little thought (for example the stimulus of a meeting a basic physical need, or responding to the demand of a boss, or reacting to something negative such as a rebuke). Furthermore I would assert that these clusters are not and cannot be scientifically defined. They represent some emerging patterns that to a degree overlap.

**Table 3.1**

The three weightings of cluster

|  | Cluster | % responses |
|---|---|---|
| Predominant group | Aspirational stimuli | 18.6% |
|  | Personal value stimuli | 12.9% |
|  | Altruistic stimuli | 11.5% |
|  | Emotional stimuli | 11.3% |
|  | Social stimuli | 8.5% |
| Middling group | Spiritual stimuli | 5.3% |
|  | Learning stimuli | 4.8% |
|  | Inspirational stimuli | 4.7% |
|  | Reward stimuli (financial) | 4.3% |
|  | Change stimuli | 4.1% |
|  | Freedom stimuli | 3.8% |
|  | Diversionary stimuli | 3.3% |
|  | Environmental stimuli | 2.6% |
|  | Discovery stimuli | 1.8% |
| Weak group | Basic stimuli | 0.9% |
|  | Demand stimuli | 0.8% |
|  | Negative stimuli | 0.8% |
|  |  | 100% |

# Key conclusions

The following are some key conclusions drawn from asking these hundreds of people the question: "What really motivates you?" The first conclusion has already been elaborated upon above. Further conclusions are summarized below and then dealt with at greater length in the following chapters.

**1 Motivational stimuli can be grouped into 17 broad clusters, of which the most important is the stimulus of aspiration**

When people talk about what motivates them there are some recurring patterns that can be described in terms of the 17 broad clusters mentioned above. One stimulus seemed to dominate and that is related to an individual's personal aspirations or what he or she wished to achieve.

## 2 Motivation is "inner energy + personal direction ➔ desired outcome"

Motivation is all to do with personal movement. The energy for that movement can be physical, emotional, intellectual or spiritual and is normally directed towards an outcome that we desire. The energy comes from within us and has to replaced from time to time as we use it up. To use the energy and to replace it, requires a stimulus drawn from one of the 17 clusters of motivational stimuli referred to above.

## 3 All motivation is self-motivation

With rare exceptions most people interviewed stated that they were self-motivated. A few thought that their boss could have an impact on their level of motivation or demotivation. However, on examination it was invariably established that the ultimate determinant was the way an individual reacted to a positive or negative behavior (or stimulus) from a boss.

## 4 All motivation is temporary

Few people are permanently motivated. Most admit to moments of demotivation when their motivational energies dip. They then have to resort to a variety of internal and external stimuli to switch back on their motivational energies

## 5 Motivation is specific not general

Motivation is not a general attribute that contributes to the characterization of a person. Motivation is a specific response to a specific stimulus (or set of stimuli) and draws upon the energies a person has and the way those energies are directed. Even so, a person's motivation can arise from a very powerful set of internal stimuli (for example, aspirational, spiritual or learning stimuli).

> *Motivation is a specific response to a specific stimulus*

## 6 People can be motivated and demotivated at the same time

Motivation is a function of energy and direction. If the directed energy meets a blockage then demotivation can occur. However, it is quite possible to redirect that energy such that a person is motivated to do something else.

Thus a person can be motivated to have a chat with their mates in the canteen at the same time as being demotivated as a result of some poor treatment they are receiving from their boss or employer.

## 7 Motivation is not the same as happiness or goodwill

Motivation is about finding the energy to do something we want. It is not the same as happiness. We can be very unhappy that a child has been hurt in an accident but very motivated to help that child. In this case motivation arises from a negative stimulus (the accident) and an altruistic stimulus (wanting to help). Similarly, motivation is not the same as goodwill. A boss can lose the goodwill of their team, which might remain motivated to do their best for each other and for their customers.

## 8 Motivation has to be stimulated – it does not happen by default

In the absence of stimulation we lose motivation and fall into "non-motivated" routines that require relatively little energy, for either thinking or feeling. Whilst in automatic mode there is little, if any, motivation or demotivation. To become motivated a stimulus is required and this can be internal (sourced from our "self") or external (sourced from outside our "self").

## 9 Logic, reason and rationales will not stimulate motivation

Nobody in the research stated that they were "motivated by reason, logic or rationales." Reason is normally exercised to moderate or control the process of motivation and the resultant behaviors, but in itself is not a stimulus to motivation. Reason is, in fact, our motive for directing our energies (whether they be physical, emotional, spiritual or intellectual) towards a specific outcome.

## 10 People are confused about "money" as a motivational stimulus

Not surprisingly a large number of people said that money did not motivate them, whilst a minority admitted to it. On examination, the stimulus in most cases was not money, but what money would bring. If what was desired could be attained without money then it was deemed that money was not a motivator. In many cases money (or salary or price) is reflection of a specific value and most people want value as well as want to be valued. Therefore a potential financial reward is a motivational stimulus, although many people would see it otherwise, discounting it in favor of higher ideals.

## 11 Motivation is largely independent of cultural differences

This is a tentative conclusion and requires further study. The people I interviewed were from around the world, including Europe, America, the Far East (Singapore and China) and Africa. The pattern of responses did not vary significantly. Irrespective of their country of origin and upbringing, most people in the world are motivated by aspiration, want to be valued, are stimulated by social contact, enjoy a positive environment and welcome change. The main differences relate to the stimulus of emotion and the stimulus of freedom. In certain cultures people struggle to see motivation in terms of putting feeling into what they do and also struggle to see it in terms of making personal choices. These cultures tend to remain autocratic with a high residue of fear in many of their organizations. They tend to be "dependency" cultures in which people depend on their bosses (or elders) to help them determine their aspirations and then also depend on their bosses to reflect personal value. In these autocratic cultures emotions are suppressed and freedoms limited and this has an impact on motivation.

In the next chapter we will take a closer look at how the stimulus factor relates to motivation.

# 4

# The stimulus factor
# and motivation

I am totally self-motivated. I generate my own motivation. It's
helped by the reaction of other people but in the end it's down
to me. I choose to be motivated. If I waited for a boss to
motivate me I'd wait until the cows came home.
*Member of hotel housekeeping staff, Singapore*

## The myth of motivation

It is incredibly patronizing to assume that one human being can motivate
another. One of the greatest myths propagated by management theorists is
that the role of a leader, or manager, is to motivate people. It is even more
dangerous to assume that companies can produce external motivational
devices (motivators) that will motivate large groups of employees.

I have in front of me a number of books on the subject of "motivating
people," all of which are based on this fallacious, albeit traditional and
patronizing, assumption. The first states
that one of the signs of demotivation is
when people do not co-operate when
extra effort is needed – when they are
reluctant to volunteer for additional
duties or when they simply avoid work (for example by dragging out coffee-
breaks). As a result it is assumed that an effective manager can come in and
motivate these demotivated people. This assumption must be challenged.

> One of the greatest myths propagated
> by management theorists is that the
> role of a leader is to motivate people

The second book I have in front of me asserts that a successful manager is one who motivates staff to achieve better results. This logic is such a part of our accepted management thinking that it is a shame to question it, but question it I will.

The third book parades all the conventions about setting goals, appraising people and empowering them, as well as how to deal with demotivated people, for example by "talking to them to identify where the problem lies and then resolving the problem." If only life at work was so simple! The fourth books goes along the same lines, spelling out such simple practices as goal setting, participation and recognition.

It is thus accepted convention that success in business stems from the ability of a manager to motivate people and that this is a key management role. Can you imagine your boss saying to you:

Well we've agreed your goals and I'm going to praise you and reward you when you achieve them. Furthermore, please come to me when you have problems and I'll do my best to support you in having them resolved. I hope you are incredibly motivated as a result!

If only motivation was that simple! It makes the basic assumption that before any manager attempts to motivate you, you must be demotivated. I have come across managers who do all the textbook things on motivation yet have incredibly demotivated people, whilst I have come across others who have no idea about the textbook but have incredibly motivated people. For example, one of our most successful entrepreneurs and inspirational leaders, Sir Richard Branson, is far from being the "product" of a business school. As he states in autobiography (1998): "I am aware that the idea of business being fun and creative goes right against the grain of convention, and it's certainly not how they teach it at some of those business schools, where business means hard grind and lots of 'discounted cash flows' and 'net present values'." Employees in the Virgin Group are motivated because of the stimulus provided by "Richard" by way of fun, creativity and inspiration. He stimulates their motivation by being himself – by being unconventional and by being very "people-oriented." In the Virgin Group there are five clusters of motivational stimuli which come to the fore: these are diversionary, inspirational and social stimuli, together with those of challenge and freedom.

Companies like those in the Virgin Group are rare however. The majority attempt to motivate people in accordance with the textbook lessons provided by business schools. The paradox is that despite all the textbooks, theories and training courses on how best to motivate people it is quite evident that in many organizations people are not motivated. This can be proved statistically through attrition rates, climate surveys, industrial relations problems, as well as through one's own anecdotal experience of dealing with disinterested and indifferent front-line people in many companies.

## All motivation is self-motivation

Something is going wrong somewhere in practising what many management experts preach. Motivating other people is not as easy as many make out. The reason is simple. It is impossible! No single person can motivate any other single person, let alone a group of people. Rather than accept this unpalatable truth, many organizations have pursued the alchemist's dream of converting demotivated people into motivated people. The alchemists are of course the so-called personnel professionals who profess to know all about motivating people and therefore seek to advise those dreadful line managers who so evidently fail to motivate anyone. (To justify their own existence, many personnel practitioners project the view that many line managers are dreadful and have no idea!) The personnel profession has claimed an expertise in motivating people which is not only of limited practical value but of limited theoretical value too. I have yet to meet a so-called personnel professional who has the ability to motivate me, let alone one who has any more expertise on motivation than the wise people you invariably find on the shop floor or in charge of it.

> Motivating other people is not as easy as many make out. The reason is simple. It is impossible!

To make the assumption that any one human being, whether that person be a chief executive officer or a team leader, can develop an ability to motivate individuals or groups of people in the organization, is equivalent to making the patronizing assumption that most people are weak of spirit, have little heart and have limited emotional strength to move them forward on a day-by-day basis. We all have soul and spirit, we all have heart and we all have emotional strength. It is just that sometimes this does not lie with the organization but elsewhere. This is then perceived as demotivation, when in fact the motivation is not directed through the workplace but beyond it.

All motivation comes from within. All motivation is self-motivation. There is no other type of motivation and to that extent "external motivation" is an illusion.

Arnie Harmsworth, one of the team leaders at WPA Medical Care Insurance who was interviewed for the research, said:

I'm self-motivated. My boss doesn't have an effect on me. He's excellent. But I'd still be motivated if he wasn't. I find it stimulating when I'm doing things I've never done before, new things. I like to use my brain. I dislike doing the same things day in and day out, repetitive work.

The motivational stimuli in this case is drawn from the clusters of change and relates to "doing new things."

None of us is an inanimate object awaiting a dose of motivation from our bosses and employers to animate us and get us moving or performing. We are already motivated and will always be motivated to a greater or lesser degree, subject to the vagaries of our moods, the ups and downs of our everyday lives and our encounters with the world beyond our immediate control. There is only one point in life when we totally lose motivation and that is at the precise end of it, when we die. Even suicidal people are motivated – to die.

> All motivation comes from within.
> All motivation is self-motivation.
> External motivation is an illusion.

As an author and speaker nobody motivates me. I am self-employed and I have no boss. All my motivation comes from within. My motivation to write this book comes from within me and derives from an aspirational stimulus. My motivation to travel to the four corners of the world to run seminars comes from within me and relates to the clusters of discovery and change. My motivation to do my very best for my clients also comes from within me and is an altruistic stimulus. My motivation to develop myself, improve myself, learn more, become wiser and apply myself more effectively comes from me. This is the learning stimulus. I have no boss to create this motivation for me.

## The impact of other people on motivation

Other people have an impact on my motivation but it is essentially *my* motivation and the way I motivate myself. The way I motivate myself draws upon my innermost spiritual, emotional and intellectual energies, as well as upon the stimuli and energies I absorb from other people and to which I respond. However, the way I respond to these external stimuli and energies (and thus behaviors of other people) is my choice. I choose how to motivate myself and I choose how to respond to other people who might even seek to motivate me. Motivation is my choice. I motivate myself. I love motivated people and their motivation sparks my own motivation. It has an impact on me. Other people can stimulate me with inspiration, enthusiasm, support, encouragement, interest, care and a range of other behavioral stimuli. However, such a stimulus will only work if I want it to work. The source of my own motivation is what I want for myself. Of course I love it when I receive positive feedback and I feel motivated as a result. But that is my choice. The positive feedback is a stimulus to my own motivation.

> The way you respond to external stimuli is your choice. Motivation is your choice. Only you can motivate yourself

There are people I know who choose not to give any motivational response to positive feedback. There were two people I interviewed with whom I was so impressed that I wanted to write them up as case studies. They refused. They did not want to be named. "We were just doing our jobs," they said. Positive feedback, either from their customers or their bosses, seemed to do nothing for them.

In other words there can be no precise prescription when it comes to stimulating motivation. One person will respond to an external stimulus totally differently from another. All we can rely on are some loose clusters of stimuli to draw upon when experimenting how best to stimulate a person motivation.

Jonathan McMillan of Schering-Plough, who was interviewed during the research for this book, said:

I am self-motivated. I don't know where motivation comes from other than from within. I work from home. I have a choice every day to get up in the morning. The bosses I've worked for – I've never regarded them as being there to motivate me. I do that myself.

In summary, motivation is our choice.

## Demotivation

The same applies to demotivation. It is a mindset we choose for ourselves. On the rare instances I feel demotivated it is because of me – it is because of the choices I make consciously or subconsciously in response to specific negative stimuli. On the few occasions I am rejected, neglected, not selected or just made to feel bad by other people it is easy to slip into a state of demotivation and blame these other people for it – to blame them for "demotivating me." But it is me who is demotivating me, not them. It is me who is blaming them. The world is not that perfect that other people will always behave in exactly the way we want them too, and it never will be. If we allow the world (or certain individuals who inhabit it) to demotivate us, that is our choice, conscious or subconscious. Whenever I receive a setback, whenever I encounter adversity – and I do from time to time – I have to dig deep into myself to draw upon my reserves of spiritual, emotional and intellectual energies to resist the temptation of "demotivation and blame." I have to convert these energies inside me into positive motivational forces, which drive me forward out of adversity and towards a more satisfactory future.

One of the people I interviewed, Jackie Matthews of HSBC, said: "I can detach myself from criticism. If I receive negative feedback, it doesn't affect my motivation. I am conscious that I must listen and accept feedback. I am conscious that I must continuously improve. It's so easy to get defensive. The challenge is to remain open always." Another interviewee, Sir Michael Bichard of the Department of Education and Employment (UK) said: "I will always deliver. My internal motivation will carry me through the most hostile terrain."

## Self-motivation in times of adversity

The bookshelves are full of stories of people who have encountered setbacks and adversity – far greater than I hope you or I will ever experience – but who, far from becoming demotivated, used these energies to motivate themselves to survive and move forward towards their desired goals. Here are two examples, the first from Joe Simpson (1988), a mountaineer who in a dreadful snowstorm plunged to near death on the side of a steep mountain. In the plunge he broke his leg and became trapped in a cave of snow with no apparent escape.

I lay face-down in the snow, unsure whether I had passed out or not. Nausea threatened to swamp up my throat, making me gasp and retch. Agony boiled from my knee … I lay back on my rucksack … I ate snow … I awoke with a start – "Get moving … don't lie there … stop dozing … move."

No matter how bad your situation, no matter how demotivated you are tempted to be, you always have a choice, either to stay still or move forward. Joe Simpson describes how he recalled some lines from Shakespeare he learnt 10 years ago: "I felt delighted and muttered the words to the silent snows around me, listening to the odd acoustics of the cave. I forgot how frightening everything was." When things are really bad you have to challenge your mindset, perhaps dig deep into your memory to recover a specific stimulus (in this case Shakespeare) to motivate yourself to move forward.

Another example is Tony Bullimore (1997), the lone sailor who spent nearly five days in icy waters sheltering in an air pocket in the upturned hull of his yacht: "I survived because I wanted to. I had no intention of going down in the Southern Ocean. It's amazing what you can achieve when you really put your mind to it!"

The point is that whatever the situation, whether or not you are up against it or even risk dying in the next half-an-hour, it is your choice whether or not to be motivated. It is no one else's choice.

## Non-motivation

In addition to motivation and demotivation there is a third state, which I call "non-motivation." This is a common occurrence in our everyday lives. In fact, for much of the time we are "non-motivated." Non-motivation exists when we do things without thinking – when we get into automatic mode, when we "tick over," when we are devoid of emotion and when we give little thought as to what to do next. It is when we go through the motions and allow habits and routines to drive our behaviors. Are we motivated as we get dressed in the morning? Are we motivated when we automatically switch on the car radio to listen to the news? Are we motivated when we park the car in the same place as yesterday? In many cases the answer is "No!" Frequently these everyday activities are undertaken without thinking, without feeling and therefore without any conscious sense of motivation or demotivation. This is "non-motivation."

## Motivation is moving towards what you want

In the end motivation is about what you want. It is to do with your personal aspirations, together with the emotional stimuli of your passions and enthusiasm. Motivation is a both a state of mind and a state of heart. It is when you consciously experience certain emotional and spiritual energies that drive you in a direction you want. Nobody can tell you what you should want. Only you can focus on what you want. Furthermore, you have to have both hope and belief that what you want will come to pass. Hope and belief are essential spiritual stimuli which are born from the depths of your soul. To quote Jung Chang (1991) who wrote so eloquently about her experiences in the Cultural Revolution in China when Mao Zedong was in power: "My job as a caster was dirty and hard. I had swollen arms from pounding the earth into the moulds, but I was in high spirits, as I believed that the Cultural Revolution was coming to an end."

Often it is your belief and spirit that stimulate the emotional energies that motivate us. Here is another example, this time from the late psychiatrist and author Viktor Frankl (1959) who survived the concentration camps in the war: "Prisoners who gave 'meaning' to their lives – perhaps simply by helping others – were themselves more likely to survive. Those who had lost any faith in the future fell into depression and were doomed."

> Motivation is about what you want. It is a both a state of mind and a state of heart.

To be motivated you must have faith in the future, you must have aspiration and you must have spirit. Demotivation is most likely to occur when you lose faith, lose hope, lose belief. Effectively when you lose your spirit your emotional energies begin to drain away, you lose heart and risk ceasing to be a human being. You just go through the physical motions of living before dying. Without aspiration, life is reduced to respiration.

My editing of this chapter has been distracted by soccer's European Cup Final on 2 July 2000. Until the last minute of injury time Italy was winning 1–0. Then, virtually with the final kick, France equalized and the game had to go into extra time. During this period France went on to win with a golden goal by David Trezeguet. To quote Roger Lemerre, France's coach: "I always say that even if we have one second remaining to play we must play at full strength" (*Daily Telegraph*, 3 July 2000).

In other words by sustaining motivation it is always possible to convert a losing situation into a winning one, even if there is only one second to go before losing. It is so easy to lose motivation when the competition is beating us, or when we are facing extreme adversity. The previous day the English cricket team came back from behind to beat the West Indies in a nail-biting finish to the second Test match.

Virtually everything is possible when you are motivated. The key is to sustain that motivation and that requires the power of both internal stimuli ("the belief that I can still win") and external stimuli ("the sound of the crowd roaring you on").

## The path of motivation

Motivation is about determining and moving towards the unique contribution we want to make (or, if selfish, take) in this world. If we simply react to the demands of others then we lose our "selves" – we become their agents rather than our "selves."

The great American intellectual Ralph Waldo Emerson (1841) wrote:

Insist on yourself, never imitate. Your own gift you can present every moment with the cumulative force of a whole life's cultivation; but of the adopted talent of another you have only an extemporaneous half-possession ... Where is the master who could have taught Shakespeare? Where is the master who could have instructed Franklin, or Washington, or Bacon, or Newton? Every great man is unique.

The Chinese American author Ching-Ning Chu (1995) would agree with Emerson: "A successful life is one that is lived through understanding and pursuing one's own path, not chasing after the dreams or fulfilling the expectations of others."

In one sense we all follow our own path in life and that is our motivation. Within the constraints that fate wraps around us we make our choices, decide upon the path and follow it. Even when we do what we are told we are deciding upon a path. Many people do not do what they are told and equally take the consequences. L. Frank Baum (1900) expressed it a different way in *The Wizard of Oz*: "'If you don't know where you are going' the Scarecrow said to Dorothy, 'it doesn't matter which road you take'."

## The internal stimulus of enthusiasm

To be motivated you must not only be clear what you want of the future (the path to take) and have the faith, hope and belief that you will achieve this, but you must also have the internal stimulus of enthusiasm. To quote Thomas J. Watson Snr from IBM speaking on the subject of motivation:

There is something which makes a man want to work. It is enthusiasm. You never saw a lazy man in your life who was enthusiastic. You never saw an enthusiastic man who was lazy. If we have enthusiasm, we want to work ... What is it that gives us enthusiasm? It is not something that you can go out and buy ... We have to do something to create enthusiasm within ourselves, that will make us want to work (Fenster, 2000).

Enthusiasm has to be stimulated either internally or externally, but essentially the energy of enthusiasm comes from within. It is an emotional energy which comes from our heart and is linked to our passions in life. There is nothing new in this: one can trace the above words of wisdom back to the Bible and the Sermon on the Mount, when Jesus said "For where your treasure is, there your heart will be also" (Matthew 6:21).

## The source of motivation

The source of our motivation is therefore what we love, what we treasure or what we passionately want of the future. It is these treasures, whether they be physical, emotional, intellectual or spiritual, that will drive us forward in life. In the workplace it begs the all-important question: "What do we really treasure?" Is it profit, revenue, statistics, data, being at the top of the league table or big fat bonuses? Or is it valuing people, serving customers and doing our best for them? Each one of us has to decide. If it is decided for us we effectively become instruments of the system and we will be in danger of allowing ourselves to lose heart.

Thus the stimuli to which we respond will be those that energize us to discover and attain what we personally treasure. We will resist those disabling stimuli that prevent us from moving towards these treasures. We will resist the boss who shouts at us or the customer who complains, unless we ourselves determine that these stimuli will enable us to move forward to our treasured goals. We will be reluctant to work with people who throw us off course, distract us or stop us from achieving what we want. We will avoid people who make us feel bad and gravitate towards people who make us feel good – if that is what we treasure in life. The challenge of motivation is to determine what makes us really feel good. Nobody else can do this for us.

> Only we as individuals can determine our own heart and thus create the emotions, passions and enthusiasms that will motivate us to move forward

Once we are clear about this we can stimulate the emotions, passions and enthusiasms which will motivate us to move forward. Gordon Bethune (1998), who had tremendous success in turning around the near bankrupt airline Continental wrote:

There's one final reason for our success. We like people and we like serving them ...
My goal, from the day I walked into Continental, was to get that sense of value into
every aspect of our operation, from the top to the bottom. I wanted every customer to
feel valued in every transaction, and every employee to feel valued every day.

What Gordon Bethune did was stimulate the desires of people in Continental to serve customers. He stimulated their sense of value by clearly articulating his own values.

During the last two days I have walked into branches of three well-known
companies which aspire to a similar set of values, yet encountered indifferent
people who were disinterested in their customers. It is not enough to declare
the value "liking people." To accomplish it – so that customers "feel it" –
companies have to generate a wide range of stimuli to energize their people.
Many still fail.

## Motivation through internal vision

The blind author and consultant Randy J. Gibbs (1998) writes of how
important "internal vision" is in being motivated. Remember that the person
writing this is blind:

How we see creates the world we experience. When we acquire greater insight, we
are able to see possibilities that we could not see before ... Deep, rich insight is
essential to increase human effectiveness and create harmony and success with
others ... The danger is we become blind to the possibilities before us and are
trapped in patterns we cannot understand and have no idea how to change. Our
internal vision becomes cloudy and filled with distortion and blind spots,
preventing us from seeing things as they really are and really can be.

In other words to be motivated we must see ahead of us the road that we
want. Only we can determine that road. Nobody can determine it for us and
that means "seeing" inside our "selves" – seeing what we really want of life
and work.

> To be motivated we must see ahead of us the road that we want. Only we can determine that road

The importance of having the
stimulus of an aspirational vision was
reinforced by three renowned musicians
who the author spoke to whilst undertaking research for the book. Howard
Shelley, the international concert pianist and conductor said, when being
interviewed on 23 July 2000 that what motivates him is to achieve the most
beautiful interpretation of the music he loves whether it be Hummel, Mozart

or Rachmaninov. When he approaches a concert he has an overall mood in mind for each phrase of the music. That is the stimulus of an aspirational vision. What do we really want of our life and work – not only in the long term but also in the short term for each daily performance?

Benjamin Zander, conductor of the Boston Philharmonic Orchestra, told the author, during a series of concerts and symposiums in Singapore between 25 and 28 August 2000, that he saw his job as helping take people out of their boxes and listen to music with their hearts as well as their minds. Part of his vision was to awaken within each member of the orchestra the possibilities of beauty and to create passionate music making without boundaries. In his book Benjamin Zander (2000) asserts that each one of us is capable of transforming our lives by harnessing the art of possibility. Such possibility arises from the stimulus of an aspirational vision.

The third musician, the Venezuelan concert pianist Elena Riu, said when interviewed on 4 March 2000: "With music I believe it is important to find your own path, a path you can have a claim too. You have to find composers you have an affinity with – instead of just following the norm. I can get a new insight into a piece of music. Sometimes you play a piece of music and you don't understand why the composer wrote it that way. Then suddenly you get the idea. This is very exciting." Here the stimulus of aspiration is combined with the stimulus of discovery.

The stimulus of an aspirational vision is equally applicable to business people as to musicians. Here is Sir Richard Branson talking, on being interviewed at his home on 22 February 2000: "I am motivated by seeing if we can do better in various types of business and then finding a team who can achieve this. Staff want to work for a company that is best, not the second best. Who wants to be second best? Everyone wants to be the best. We want staff who are proud to work for Virgin because it is the best. What motivates me is that I am in a position that I'm still achieving things I'm proud of. I like to enable other people to challenge themselves in the same way as I challenge myself. I want Virgin to be an example of not what we say but of what we do. I believe you have to get the people thing right, then the customer service follows and then the profit. I've always liked people and I think this is essential for business. My parents always looked for the best in people – and they looked for the best in me. That's how I learnt."

It is quite clear from the research that successful people motivate themselves through the stimulus of internal aspiration. This has nothing to do with where you come from and whether you are British (Sir Richard Branson, Howard Shelley), American (Benjamin Zander, Randy Gibbs) or

Venezuelan (Elena Riu). All motivated people, whether front line and unknown or at the forefront of their art and well known, are those who have determined their own path in life by virtue of a powerful personal vision.

We cannot go through life with a navigator sitting alongside us and instructing us where to go. A boss cannot do that for us and nor can anybody else. At times we will need the stimulus of advice and support from others and at other times we will need to draw upon the energies of others, but in the end nobody can determine for us the choices we have to make in life on how to expend our own energies. Motivation is the determination of how we, as unique human beings, should spend our own energies. At worst a dictator can force us under threat of death to expend physical energy, but what a dictator cannot do is force us to expend our own person emotional, intellectual and spiritual energies.

We can always, if we choose, retain the latter energies within the privacy of our own "self" and use them sparingly for our "self" and when appropriate for those we love, trust and want to help. The old saying: "You can lead a horse to water but you cannot make it drink" is equally applicable in the workplace and motivation. Therefore no boss can force us to smile at a customer or invest emotional energy in developing relationships with clients. At worst a boss can force us to do the bare minimum physical work for which we are paid. At best a boss will spark the immense reserves of motivational energy we have within us so that we move in the desired direction.

## Not being motivated is not the same as being demotivated

It is an illusion to believe that you can take a team of people and motivate them to climb Mount Everest. They will only climb Mount Everest if they want to. Personally, I do not want to and therefore I am not motivated to do so. However, because I am not motivated to climb Mount Everest does not mean that I am demotivated. Not being motivated is *not* the same as being demotivated.

Similarly, it is an illusion to believe that you can take a team of people and motivate them to produce their best results ever for the department. Just because they are not motivated to produce their best results for you does not mean that they are demotivated. It just means they are not motivated to do their best for the department. They might well be motivated to do their best for each other but not for you. People will only produce their best results if *they* want to – not because you want them to. To that extent it is their decision as to what they mean by "the best" and whether or not they want to achieve it. Most people are motivated to do their best for their families.

To quote two airline staff I interviewed at Heathrow: "We've always been motivated. What our Chief Executive did was kill the goodwill. He didn't support us, he twisted the knife in and screwed it around. However, that hasn't stopped us from being motivated to do our best for our customers."

You can attempt to excite people, inspire them, enthuse them and encourage them in an attempt to stimulate their interest in climbing Mount Everest (achieving their best results ever) but this will be to no avail unless *they* genuinely want to. It is *their* motivation, with your support, that will lead them to climb the mountain and achieve their best results ever. Expressed another way, you can try to stimulate another person's intrinsic motivation but you cannot create that intrinsic motivation for them. Thus you could stimulate my intrinsic motivation to speak at a conference in New York, but you could never motivate me to abseil down the side of the Empire State Building, even if you paid me a million!

> The source of our motivation lies in our hearts

The source of all motivation therefore lies within the self. It is seated within the soul and the heart and has to be liberated by a process of stimulation exercised through our conscious intellect, with the help of a variety of external stimuli.

## The stimulus–motivation sequence

The word "motivation" derives from the Old French word *movere* meaning "to move," which itself derives from the Latin word *motivus*. The word "motivation" has the same root therefore as the words "motive," "motor" and "motion." Furthermore, the word "motivation" has the same root as the word "emotion." So motivation is all to do with the reasons ("motives") for moving ("motion") in a certain direction and is closely connected with how we feel ("emotion"). The source of our motivation thus lies in our hearts, from which our emotions emerge. Emotions are our response to feelings. In turn, feelings relate to the detection of internal and external stimuli. The sequence (stimulus → feelings → emotions → motivation → behavior) is what I call the "stimulus–motivation sequence." It can be illustrated by the following example:

- **Situation** – I am a mother sitting at home reading a paper. My two-year-old daughter is playing nearby.

- **Stimulus (detected by my eyes and ears)** – My two-year-old daughter falls over, hurts herself and starts screaming.

- **Feeling** – I feel guilty. I was attending to my own selfish interests (reading a paper), wasn't watching, didn't protect her, didn't explain to her to take better care.

- **Emotions** – Guilt, alarm, care, love.

- **Motivation (what I want – to feel good)** – To ease her pain, to show her my love, to care for her, to help her learn the lesson.

- **Clusters of motivational stimuli** – Emotional, altruistic, social, learning.

- **Behavior** – I pick her up, cuddle her, reassure her, examine her, massage her knees and hands which have been hurt.

In this example it is not the daughter who is motivating the mother but the mother who is motivated to cuddle her daughter as a result of the external "scream stimulus," together with the internal stimulus of "wanting to care." In this sequence our psychological filtering process allows in (rather than screens out) a small parcel of energy (the stimulus of a scream) to stimulate our feelings. As our feelings are aroused, emotions quickly emerge which motivate us in the direction we want – to ease our daughter's pain. Our subsequent physical behavior results from this motivation.

The same sequence can be applied to virtually every human situation including business and management. Here is just one illustration from the workplace:

- **Situation** – I am behind schedule working on an urgent report that must be completed by the end of the day.

- **Stimulus (detected by my eyes and ears)** – The phone rings at exactly the same time as my boss approaches me waving a piece of paper.

- **Feeling** – I feel stressed. The last thing I want is these further interruptions.

- **Emotions** – Irritation, uncertainty, worry, some anger.

- **Motivation (what I want – to feel good)** – To deal with the interrupts as quickly and politely as possible so that I can return to my urgent report.

- **Clusters of motivational stimuli** – Aspirational, emotional (negative).

- **Behavior** – Signal to my boss to wait a minute whilst I pick up the phone.

▷ **Fresh stimulus** – I pick up the phone and find it is an important customer who wants to confirm an order which has been much delayed, although it has now come through for a substantially increased volume of work.

▷ **New feelings** – I feel relieved we have won the order as I had given up hope and feared we had lost it to a competitor.

▷ **New emotions** – Delight, optimism, confidence, hope.

▷ **New motivation (what I want – to feel good)** – To tell the world we've won this order, to celebrate with the team, to re-prioritize my work so that I can get to work on processing the order.

▷ **Clusters of new motivational stimuli** – Fresh aspirations, social, diversionary, emotional (positive).

▷ **Behavior** – Inform my boss who is standing by me that we've got the order and show him my delight. Propose to him that we have a small celebration for the team at lunch time. Propose to him that the completion of my urgent report be delayed by one day. Remember to listen! When my boss approached me a minute ago what did he want? Ask him.

In this example the source of motivation is not the boss, nor even the customer, but initially an individual's intrinsic emotional need to relieve some stress by completing an urgent report and subsequently that individual's emotional response to some good news. In other words it is our emotions that drive our motivation towards what makes us feel good. These emotions and feelings can be evoked by any one or more of the vast array of stimuli that rain down on us every day. We screen out most of these stimuli, but through the conscious and subconscious processes taking place in our brain we permit certain high-priority stimuli to permeate our defenses and stimulate our feelings and emotions. This in turn leads to our motivation to behave and even think in a certain type of way in response to such stimuli. As previously stressed, some of the high-priority stimuli can be generated internally from the spirit in our soul. In other words, occasionally we have to dig deep into our innermost reserves of spiritual energies to trigger our motivation.

> To understand motivation we have to understand ourselves

To understand motivation, therefore, we have to understand ourselves and why we respond in specific ways to different types of external and internal stimuli. It means we have to understand and develop our own personal philosophies which comprise the values, beliefs and principles that not only condition our emotional and intellectual responses to external stimuli and but are also the source of the internal stimuli that trigger our motivation to achieve certain things in life.

## The binary code of motivation

These internal stimuli derive from the most basic mechanism of human survival, which I describe as the "binary code" of motivation.

The choices we make as human beings, and thus our most basic motivations, are simple. With rare exceptions we will do one of two things in pursuing every single stimulus–motivation sequence in every day of our lives. We will either:

▷ move away from what will make us feel bad, or

▷ move towards what will make us feel good.

Everything we do in our life is based on this binary code. When we receive a negative stimulus (for example, we see someone we don't like in the distance) we are motivated to move away to minimize the possibility of us feeling bad. Conversely, when we receive a positive stimulus (for example we see a loved one in the distance) we are motivated to move in that person's direction to make us feel good.

The driving force in applying this binary code is our desire for a sense of well-being; it is all to do with making us *feel* good and not *feel* bad. Feelings are closely connected with emotions and are to do with the sensations we experience in response to various stimuli. These sensations (feelings) in turn trigger emotions that move us (or motivate us to move) in a certain direction. That direction is always towards making us feel good. This is the prime motivation in life. The binary code effectively represents the two opposite "poles" of existence.

As spiritual human beings with deep-rooted souls (and this goes back to Adam and Eve) we are continually faced with individual choices to determine what makes us feel good and feel bad and to move in the appropriate direction. The choices are complex and life is all about navigating a tortuous path through these conflicting choices ( of what is "good and bad" vs. "what makes us feel good and what makes us feel bad"). We are faced with such choices every day. Logic would dictate that what is "good" should make us "feel good." However, as imperfect human beings we all know it is not as simple as that.

## Reward psychology

Much of our motivation to "feel good" is based on what is called "reward psychology" – whether that reward be physical, emotional, intellectual or spiritual. Paradoxically, many of the stimuli that make us feel good in the short term can make us feel bad in the long term, for example alcohol, drugs, unhealthy nutrition, lack of exercise and general sloth.

To discover our "selves" as human beings and thus our own sources of self-motivation we have to examine all these conflicting options and attempt to make behavioral choices that will make us feel good in the long term but not necessarily in the short term. This is the struggle. In a world of instant availability the motivation of instant gratification is in danger of corrupting the soul as we strive, with ease, to meet our selfish desires. The issue of motivation thus ceases to be an external one, in which we seek to motivate other people, but an internal one, in which we struggle to choose between conflicting long-term and short-term desires. In others words, self-motivation is often a battle to choose personal behaviors in response to a wide range of conflicting stimuli. The battle can only be won (or lost) by our "self." It is not just a matter of choosing to be motivated, but choosing in which areas we want to be motivated.

# The four main areas of motivation

Perhaps this presents us with the biggest challenge we find in life. The newspapers are littered with stories of people who fall foul of society by failing to control effectively their motivation for instant gratification. As individuals we therefore have to determine for ourselves the higher level goals, which go beyond instant gratification and which we will be motivated to achieve. This requires serious examination and consideration of what we really want in life. We want to feel good, but the real struggle is to determine what will actually make us feel good amongst the thousands of opportunities presented to us daily.

This sense of well-being or feeling good derives progressively from the following four main areas of motivation:

▶ **Body** – Physically feeling good (e.g. pleasant physical sensations).

▶ **Heart** – Emotionally feeling good (e.g. feeling happy).

▶ **Mind** – Intellectually feeling good (e.g. a sense of achievement).

▶ **Soul** – Spiritually feeling good (e.g. acting with integrity).

Table 4.1 provides some examples of these four areas of motivation. (Note that one could equally devise the four main areas of demotivation.) Each of the examples of a stimulus can be related to one of the 17 clusters.

**Table 4.1**

**The four main areas of motivation**

| Motivation area (wanting to ...) | Category (examples) | Stimulus (examples) |
| --- | --- | --- |
| Physically feel good or have pleasant sensations (body) | Taste | Eating chocolate |
| | Smell | Perfume |
| | Sight | A beautiful landscape |
| | Sound | Chopin |
| | Touch | Hot fluffy towels |
| | Activity | Exercise |
| Emotionally feel good or feel happy (heart) | Joy | Son passes examinations |
| | Excitement | Attending a football match |
| | Love | Family reunion |
| | Amusement | Comedy film |
| | Kindness | Visiting a sick person |
| Intellectually feel good or sense achievement (brain) | Problem solving | Crossword puzzles |
| | Acquiring knowledge | Becoming an expert |
| | Challenge | Obtaining qualifications |
| | Curiosity | Discovering new thinking |
| | Science | Learning how things work |
| Spiritually feel good or acquire wisdom (soul) | Principles | Practising: honesty, trust |
| | Beliefs | Applying: religion, philosophy |
| | Values | Practising: giving, caring |
| | Awareness | Receiving and accepting feedback |
| | Improvement | Self-development, positive thinking |

A sense of well-being, a sense of feeling good, and a sense of being motivated can arise from any combination of the above. Thus we can feel good both physically and emotionally at the same time. Our "self" coalesces these various specific feelings (deriving from physical, emotional, intellectual and spiritual stimuli) into an overall feeling which can be good, bad or just "ordinary."

Furthermore, it is quite possible to feel good and feel bad at the same time. In the first example the taste of chocolate can stimulate a person to feel good at the same time as the consumption of the bar makes them feel guilty or bad. The impact of a stimulus can never be more than temporary, whilst an excess of one type of stimuli will soon flip us into feeling bad. Even when it comes to the power of the aspiration, different stimuli need to be used to sustain the motivation. Repeated application of one type of aspirational stimulus will always lead to disappointment. At one stage in the award-winning film *American Beauty* the "heroine" Carolyn Burnham (played by Annette Bening) repeatedly thumps her chest and screams to herself "I am going to be successful today!" – but to little effect. If one aspirational stimulus is not effective, another fresh one has to be found.

> All motivation is temporary and to regain it a further stimulus is required

Table 4.2 provides a set of examples from the workplace. Again, one could equally devise the four main areas of demotivation.

## The psychogenetics of motivation

Each of us as a unique human being will have a different profile of motivation in terms of what makes us feel good. This is what I describe as the "psychogenetics" of motivation. In the same way that our physical characteristics are unique and derive from our genetic make-up and a unique combination of 23 chromosomes, our motivational make-up is also unique and derives from a unique set of "motivational drivers" or "psychogenes" that are embedded in our hearts, bodies, minds and souls. Whilst we find it impossible to change our genetic make-up (although scientists are trying hard to do so) it is debatable as to the extent to which we are born with a fixed set of motivational drivers and to what extent these can be modified by external stimuli (the environment) and internal stimuli (our "selves").

Thus the motivational drivers (or psychogenes) for a monk will be totally different to those of a nuclear physicist or an actor. For a monk honouring a vow of silence, the motivation of spiritually feeling good will be dominant. For a nuclear physicist, the dominant motivational force might be intellectually feeling good, whilst for an actor it could be emotionally feeling good.

## Table 4.2

The four main areas of motivation in the workplace

| Motivation area (wanting to ...) | Category (examples) | Stimulus (examples) |
|---|---|---|
| Physically feel good or have pleasant sensations (body) | Taste | Freshly brewed coffee |
| | Smell | Flowers in reception |
| | Sight | Decorations in office |
| | Sound | Silence |
| | Touch | Comfortable seating |
| | Activity | Getting up, moving around |
| Emotionally feel good or feel happy (heart) | Delight | Colleague announces pregnancy |
| | Excitement | Winning a major order |
| | Warmth | Social gathering |
| | Fun | Office quiz |
| | Kindness | Visiting a sick colleague |
| Intellectually feel good or sense achievement (brain) | Problem solving | Cracking a quality problem |
| | Acquiring knowledge | Becoming an expert on IT |
| | Challenge | Completing a project on time |
| | Curiosity | Discovering new thinking |
| | Technology | Learning how system works |
| Spiritually feel good or acquire wisdom (soul) | Principles | Practising: honesty, trust |
| | Beliefs | Applying: personal credo at work |
| | Values | Practising: giving, caring |
| | Awareness | Receiving and accepting feedback |
| | Improvement | Self-development, positive thinking |

For most people, however, the "psychogenetic" profile of motivation is spread across each of the four main areas, albeit with different degrees of importance. The requirement for stimuli will therefore relate to the importance to an individual of wanting to feel good in that area of motivation. We can thus change our motivation by changing what is important to us in life and therefore by changing the way we react to motivational stimuli such as chocolate, fun, intellectual challenge and altruistic endeavour. For some people the taste stimulus of chocolate has a high degree of importance in their motivation profile, whilst for others it has little importance. For many people the fun stimulus of a party on Friday night tends to be the driving force for all their motivation, whilst for others fun has little importance. For some people the intellectual challenge of a crossword puzzle stimulates their motivation, whilst for people like me it has no importance at all. Another example is the minority of individuals for whom the altruistic stimulus of helping people is incredibly important whilst the majority are much more selfish.

Figure 4.1 gives an example of a psychogenetic motivation profile of a certain front-line service provider I know (who has asked to remain anonymous).

The main psychogenetic motivation areas in this case are:

- **body** – food
- **heart** – kindness
- **soul** – integrity and altruism.

No value judgment should be placed on this profile. Sports people will score high on the motivation to feel good physically, whilst actors will be motivated by emotionally feeling good. Scientists will score high on the intellectual motivators whilst religious elders will be motivated towards feeling good spiritually.

We all have different "motivation profiles" and we can all change these profiles by a process of internal stimulation (intellectually, emotionally and

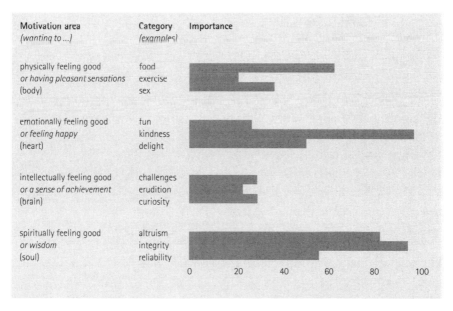

### Fig 4.1

Psychogenetic motivation profile

spiritually) to review what is really important to us in life. What do we really want in life? Have we really got the balance right at this point of time? I heard a story on the radio of a business executive who had just retired and who had spent the last 40 years totally consumed in his career and work – at the expense of his family. Now by way of compensation he was devoting much of his time to his grandchildren, although he still harbored regrets about neglecting his wife, son and daughter who had stood by him all this time.

> It is critical that we review our own "motivation profile" on a regular basis

It is critical that we review our own "motivation profile" on a regular basis especially in relation to our work and the way we manage employees You might ask yourself the following questions:

▷ What do I really want of my work that will make me feel good? (i.e. What are the aspirations that stimulate me?)

▷ What is my "motivation profile" in terms of wanting to feel good physically, emotionally, intellectually and spiritually at work?

These questions also have immense implications for the way we deal with employees and customers in each of our businesses. Again, you might ask yourself the following questions:

▷ What does a customer (or employee) really want of my company (or organization) that really makes him or her feel good?

▷ What is the "motivation profile" of a customer in terms of wanting to feel good physically, emotionally, intellectually and spiritually when dealing with my company?

The answers to these questions will help you review and possibly change the stimuli that are currently used in sparking not only your own motivation but possibly the internal motivation of customers and employees.

For example, one of the people interviewed for the research, Richard Killoran, General Manager of Austin Reed's flagship store in Regent Street, London, tells of an occasion when a customer came in to buy a suit and a couple of shirts. The store assistant sensed that the customer was highly stressed and was in a hurry. This stimulated the assistant to enquire politely a little more about the rush to buy such an important piece of clothing. The customer explained that his car was parked on a meter nearby and his time was about to expire. He feared being clamped. The assistant asked the customer in which street the car was parked and the number of the car. He then took some £1 coins from the till, excused himself for five minutes (whilst the customer tried on further clothes) and went and fed the meter. The customer was delighted, and with more time at hand purchased additional clothing.

The lessons are clear by using the stimulus–motivation sequence:

▶ **Stimulus** – A customer's highly stressed behavior.

▶ **Feeling** – Concern for the customer.

▶ **Emotion** – Care, excitement (opportunity to help), concern.

▶ **Motivation (what I want – to feel good)** – To take an initiative to please the customer (to make the customer feel good).

▶ **Clusters** – Altruistic + inspirational (creative) + emotional.

▶ **Behavior** – Determine why customer is stressed and take appropriate action.

The binary code of motivation can also be applied to this example:

▶ the customer wanted to move away from feeling bad (stress relating to expiring time on parking meter);

▶ the customer want to move towards feeling good (purchasing and wearing smart new high-quality clothes).

The stimulus for the store attendant was the stressed behavior of the customer which motivated the attendant to take action to eliminate the bad feeling and enhance the good feeling. The customer's internal motivation to purchase was stimulated by the behavior of the store assistant.

## The impact of food on motivation

A contributory factor to our position along the demotivation–motivation spectrum and our sense of well-being is the impact of certain foods and nutrients on our moods and energy levels. For example, is well known that an excess of cola can make some kids go "hyper" and that Attention Deficit Disorder (ADD) can be exacerbated by specific foods. There is sufficient evidence (Khalsa, 1997; Pert, 1997 ), that certain foods can have a positive or negative impact on our motivation by stimulating the release of various types of hormones and neurochemicals (such as scrotonin) into our body. According to a news report in the *Sunday Times* (Waterhouse, 2000):

73

Researchers have identified an area of the brain called the basal ganglia as one that is particularly involved in the stimulation we receive from food and drugs such as nicotine and alcohol. The brain has an absolutely fabulous system for getting reward signals. In order to break the cycle and trick it into not wanting more of the (unhealthy, bad) stimulus, it should be given another type of reward.

However it would be unwise to deduce that all motivation and behavior can be influenced by the food we eat, although it can be a factor in certain situations. We are not driven by the food we eat but by our emotions, intellects and spirits which, if strong enough, can override the negative impact of bad foods and ideally resist them.

# Negative stimuli

One of the important clusters of motivational stimuli relates to negativity and the experiences we have in life when we encounter adversity, when things go wrong and when people abuse us or treat us unfairly.

When people become demotivated it is invariably in response to such negative stimuli. However, because people choose their level of motivation it does not follow that all people become demotivated in response to a given negative stimulus. For many people a negative stimulus, such as a failure or a loss, is an incredibly powerful motivational stimulus. To quote one of the interviewees, Lisa Greaves of HSBC: "I'm lucky I've never been in a position where I've been demotivated. It was the way I was raised. I was raised in a positive household. I was taught to pick myself up, dust myself down and carry on if I was knocked down."

Negative stimuli can be either internal or external.

## Internal negative stimuli

The internal negative stimuli arise when we just feel down-at-heart, low-in-spirit, flat or depressed and when we seem to lack the motivation and energy to pursue activities which we normally enjoy. This can happen to us all and can result from tiredness, overindulgence or a range of other factors. It can be addressed by tapping into the strength of our spirits to elicit positive internal stimuli and/or exposing ourselves to positive external stimuli (such as music or friendly encouraging people). These will help us unleash new motivational energies to override the negativity.

## External negative stimuli

Demotivation also frequently occurs in response to negative *external* stimuli.

One of the important clusters of motivational stimuli relates to negativity and the experiences we have in life when we suffer setbacks, when things go wrong, or when people abuse us or treat us unfairly.

Something happens to us (or does not happen) that we feel bad about and makes us demotivated as a result. It occurs when we lose out, fail, have bad experiences or when our desires and expectations are not met. It is when our movement towards feeling good is impeded by unforeseen circumstances or what we perceive as the bad behavior of others. It occurs when we have setbacks. It might be failing a driving test, or when our boss shouts at us, or when we do not get the pay rise we expect. It might be caused by a persistent "bitchy" atmosphere in the office or a continual lack of recognition of all the hard work we are putting in. It might occur when we are ignored by a certain person or when we receive a complaint from a customer.

Demotivation and motivation are the two poles at the end of a continuous spectrum, as shown in Fig. 4.2. Unless we suffer from clinical depression (a physical condition), a state of demotivation will eventually lead to a state of motivation. Demotivated people will invariably be motivated to move away from feeling bad and move towards feeling good. Both states are temporary and we all, with rare exceptions, experience periods of both demotivation and motivation, as well as extended periods of non-motivation when we are totally unaware of whether we are motivated or demotivated.

> Even the most motivated people experience occasional failures that set them back on their heels with feelings of demotivation

No matter how highly motivated we are we cannot sustain that level of motivation without a fresh stimulus. In the absence of such a stimulus there will be an erosion or decay in our motivation. This is reflected in the "stimulus curve," shown in Fig. 4.3.

Nobody can sustain a peak of motivation for too long before an erosion or decay surreptitiously takes place. The motivational peaks therefore have to be regenerated with fresh positive stimuli. They also have to protected from the potentially accelerating impact of negative stimuli, which speed up the downward decline. For example, you might find your work increasingly repetitive and boring (downward decline into demotivation), and then your boss comes along and criticizes you unfairly, thus accelerating the decline towards a nadir of demotivation.

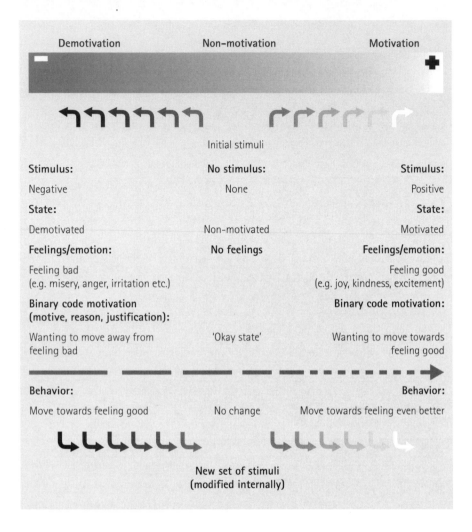

**Fig 4.2**

The demotivation–motivation spectrum

The stimulus curve in Fig. 4.3 is purely diagrammatic and the levels of demotivation, motivation and non-motivation which are experienced in the ups and downs of everyday life will vary from person to person. However, it is a rare to find a person who is motivated all the time and equally rare to find a person who is demotivated all the time. Even the most motivated people experience occasional failures that set them back on their heels with feelings of demotivation. These are the times when nothing seems to go right.

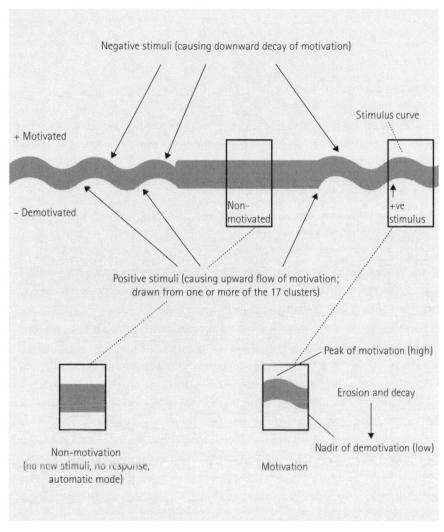

**Fig 4.3**

The stimulus curve: the up and down flows from being demotivated to motivated

Furthermore unless we pay attention to the way we motivate ourselves internally there is a risk that motivation decays (as indicated in the stimulus curve), our consciously motivated behaviors drift into routine and mediocrity and we become non-motivated, before we eventually succumb to the demotivated states of boredom, indifference and negativity. Thus we constantly need to stimulate our own motivation, as well as attempt to stimulate the motivation of others.

A report in *The Sunday Times* (Pearce, 2000) recently stated:

When the British film director Anthony Minghella won an Oscar for *The English Patient* he began to have doubts ... "I feel strongly that I want people to appreciate that I am not just a flash in the pan" he said in relation to his masterly new film *The Talented Mr Ripley*.

Motivation is ongoing, not static. A peak is reached, success is achieved (in this case an Oscar), but then the decline begins and needs to be arrested. For Anthony Minghella the Oscar was the stimulus for a further motivational force to prove to the world that he was not just a flash in the pan.

## Motivation is a flow towards the future

Thus the process of motivation, demotivation and non-motivation is actually a continual flow through time. When we experience motivation we have a flow of energies that directs our behavior towards what we want. When we achieve this and feel good, the flow continues and we are motivated to achieve something further for the future. For example, we might be motivated to earn a large incentive bonus at the end the year. When we achieve this we find we have further motivations, such as to spend this money on some wonderful vacation on an exotic paradise island, or to purchase a lovely new home or a dream car. When we eventually take the vacation, purchase the home and drive the car we find that they no longer satisfy us and that we have a fresh set of motivations. We want to return to the paradise island next year, we want to show all our friends our new home, we want to use the car to drive up into the mountains or visit our kids at university. Our motivation goes on and on in response to what we want of the future and is thus stimulated by our aspirations and innermost drives, as well as by the events that happen to us in everyday life.

In everyday life we encounter other people, such as colleagues and bosses, who can have a positive or negative impact on our own internal levels of motivation. Their behaviors can be inspirational and stimulate our emotions and motivation or they can be discouraging and suppress our emotions and motivation. When we experience these negative external stimuli we have to draw upon our reserves of emotional, intellectual and spiritual energies to resist the potential demotivation and thus use internal stimuli to remotivate ourselves. In the same way that our immune system internally creates antibodies to fight an infection caused by an external pathogenic agent, our own motivation system needs to create internal stimuli to resist the potential damage of demotivation caused by negative external stimuli, as well as select positive external stimuli to counteract them.

# 5

## The stimulated self

The more stimulating you are as a person, the more likely
you are to develop stimulating relationships with other people.

## Stimulating your own intellect, emotions and spirit

Mastering the stimulus factor in practice will help you achieve whatever you
want in life and at work. The ability to stimulate your own intellect,
emotions and spirit is critical to your own personal development, as well as
to the way you stimulate positive relationships with other people. The more
stimulating you are as a person, the more likely you are to develop stimulating relationships with other people, as well as stimulate the actions needed
to bring you the success you desire.

Every single person in this world is unique and this is manifest not only
through our physical looks but also through our souls, hearts and minds. To
make progress in life it is critical that this uniqueness is developed, so that
we create an identity that is distinct from any other person. A failure to
develop such uniqueness will lead to conformity by which we unwittingly
adopt the thinking and behaviors of others. In this way we tend to lose some
of our identity and acquire "labels" assigned to us by various social
groupings. These labels are frequently political or religious, but can also be
more local and relate to the company for which we work or the school to
which we went.

The erosion of individual identity leads to us becoming lost in the crowd
and makes us unable to set ourselves apart when need be. That need is most

important in a competitive situation, for example when looking for a job, when going for promotion, when trying to sell something or when trying to establish a business. Why you, when you are no different from the rest?

## Stimulating your own unique identity

The most stimulating people are those who constantly challenge themselves to discover and develop their own unique identity. A high degree of self-awareness is one of the most valuable attributes that any person can acquire in life. By being able to see yourself for what you really are puts you in a more powerful position to respond to others, who will also see you for what you are.

> The most stimulating people are those who are constantly challenging themselves to discover and develop their own unique identity

Conversely, those people who have a low degree of self-awareness tend to behave in a way that alienates others, unaware of the negative impact of their behavior.

To quote Robin Skynner (1993) in a conversation with John Cleese "I saw with inescapable clarity how everything we do affects other people, and how little I was aware of the effects, and how much harm that unawareness does to others."

People who have a low degree of self-awareness entrap their minds, hearts and spirits within the limited boundaries of their own opinions and feelings. They tend to be unresponsive to stimuli beyond these boundaries. As such, these people become opinionated, frequently go into denial mode and fail to tolerate others whose opinions and feelings do not fall within the same boundaries. Alienation occurs, with the resultant limited progress in life. These are the people (and many of us are like this) who are obsessed with their own thing. They are not interested in anybody else or anything else except what falls within the narrow boundaries of their own limited life. These boundaries enclose interests such as work, family, friends and their own personal activities (such as sport or shopping). These people are totally indifferent and unresponsive to anything or anybody outside these boundaries (see Fig. 5.1).

The key to developing one's self-awareness, therefore, is to develop an acute personal sensitivity as to the various types of stimuli one seeks out and responds to within and outside existing boundaries. It means questioning the whole concept of "oneself" and allowing one's heart, mind and spirit to be

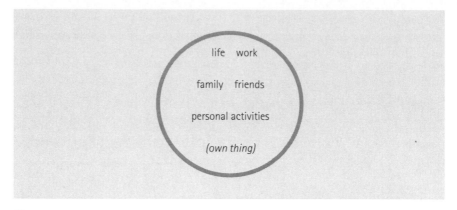

**Fig 5.1**

The narrow boundary of people obsessed with 'their own thing'

touched by a wide range of stimuli. In other words, the "stimulated self" is a self in which the heart is regularly stimulated along with the intellect and the spirit. To do this one has to push back the boundaries of one's life by allowing into it new people and fresh experiences (*see* Fig. 5.2).

## Stimulating your soul

The pure center of the "self" is the soul, in which is vested our unique spirit as individual human beings. However, the soul cannot see "itself" for what it is. We therefore need to use the feelings and thoughts generated by our hearts and minds to examine and develop our souls and to discover and improve our selves. In other words, the process of "soul discovery" or "self-discovery" (along with "spiritual development" or "self-development") cannot be generated from within the "self" but only by the process of stimulating the soul, using the heart and mind as catalysts. By this process of self-stimulation we posit in the soul an increasing number of basic truths and essential wisdoms that we believe will hold us in good stead for making our way in the world. The normal human tendency to neglect spiritual development (by failing to stimulate our souls) means that these basic truths, essential wisdoms and intrinsic beliefs increasingly become obscured and as a result we get thrown off-course in life.

> The soul cannot see "itself" for what it is

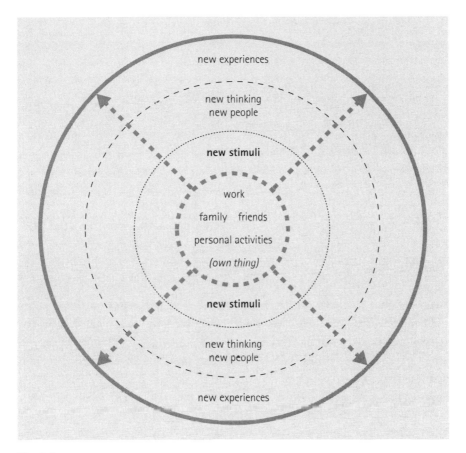

new experiences

new thinking
new people

**new stimuli**

work

family   friends

personal activities

*(own thing)*

**new stimuli**

new thinking
new people

new experiences

**Fig 5.2**
Pushing back the boundaries to become a stimulated self

## The stimulus of "imagination" and "talking to ourselves"

This process of self-discovery is not as strange as it might appear. Most people would confess to "talking to themselves" and being able to "imagine" future possibilities. What is going on when we "talk to ourselves" is a dialogue between the conscious mind and the soul (our "self") about our past experiences and our fantasies of the future, with a view to identifying what behavioral steps we should take next. Through this internal dialogue we are effectively using our brain to stimulate our hearts and souls to produce interpretations of the past which will help us develop a guide to our future behavior. Without this ability to "talk to ourselves" and "imagine things" we would be mere animals.

In fact, what we denote as "thinking" is this process of "talking to ourselves" and "imagination." Most of our mental energy is spent "talking to ourselves" about the future and/or "imagining' it. Whilst our hearts create the passions that drive our behaviors, our brain seeks to moderate these passions and the desired behaviors by referring them to the wisdom of the soul. This process is what we call "thinking" or "talking to ourselves." Rationality is the justification of our drives and behaviors, following the conscious intervention of our mind. Ideally we should establish before the event "pre-rationalities" of our drives and behaviors before we actually initiate them. Regrettably, in too many instances we try to explain away our behaviors after the event by using "afterthoughts" or concocted "post-rationalities." It would seem that the powerful passions that reside in our hearts often conspire with the brain to deceive our selves to allow behaviors that conflict with the resident wisdom in our souls.

> Rationality is the justification of the drives that emanate from our hearts and souls

To become a stimulated self we thus need constantly to stimulate our hearts, minds and souls to develop and reinforce the essential wisdoms and passions for a successful life, whilst flushing away the dangerous deceits, conceits and delusions that we often misguidedly posit in our hearts. It is an ongoing cyclical process by which our hearts, minds and soul constantly stimulate each other with lively interactive debate on "what can I learn about the past and what is the best course of action for me to take now?" (*see* Fig. 5.3).

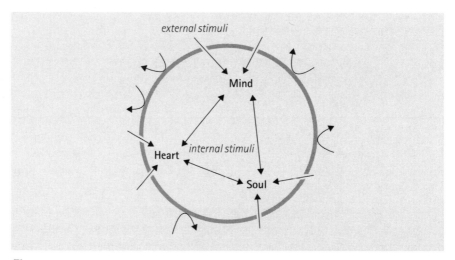

**Fig 5.3**

The stimulated self

The cyclical process of internal stimulation is accentuated by the addition of selected external stimuli. The constant process of stimulation thus keeps our minds, hearts and souls active such that we become a stimulated self. By closing our minds, by closing off our hearts and by suppressing our souls, we deny ourselves essential stimulation. The start point for developing a stimulated self is to use a conscious stimulus from our mind to trigger an ongoing process of internal stimulation. An external stimulus (such as a moment of inspiration) can be used to trigger this conscious process. Thus a quote from a brilliant speech might be the external stimulus that "makes us think" and starts the process of internal stimulation in which we re-activate our hearts and souls and examine the emotional and spiritual impact they have on our behaviors. As Confucius said: "The gold in our heart is more precious than the gold in our purse." So we need to let the pure gold that is at the center of each one of us as individuals shine through in our everyday behaviors. Do some good today, give something good from yourself to another.

The practical outcomes of developing a stimulated self are given in Table 5.1.

**Table 5.1**

Practical outcomes of developing a stimulated self

| The stimulated self | Practical outcomes (examples) |
|---|---|
| The stimulated heart | Demonstrable enthusiasms<br>Positive feelings always evident |
| The stimulated spirit | Personal values and beliefs shine through<br>At one with oneself and others |
| The stimulated mind | Communicates with imagination<br>Always curious, always learning |

# Developing a stimulated self

There are eight practical steps that can be used in developing a stimulated self and thus become a stimulating person.

## 1 Establish your own psychogenetic motivational profile

Referring to the previous two chapters, establish an outline profile of yourself in terms of what really motivates you and the stimuli that are need for this. Firstly, review the 17 clusters of motivational stimuli and ask yourself: "Which of these is really important to me in terms of my own motivation?"

As a reminder, the list of 17 clusters are:

Cluster 1     **Aspirational stimuli** – Hopes, dreams, challenges, vision, goals, mission, achievement, success, winning, etc.

Cluster 2     **Learning stimuli** – Self-improvement, personal development, knowledge etc.

Cluster 3     **Discovery stimuli** – Revelation, curiosity, questioning etc.

Cluster 4     **Diversionary stimuli** – Fun, entertainment, games, sport, distraction etc.

Cluster 5     **Reward stimuli – financial and related** – Incentives, prizes, awards, pay, bonuse etc.

Cluster 6     **Personal value stimuli** – Appreciation, recognition, being valued etc.

Cluster 7     **Inspirational stimuli** – Art, music, writing, creativity, "eureka" moments, brainwaves etc.

Cluster 8     **Altruistic stimuli** – Care, giving, doing good, philanthropy etc.

Cluster 9     **Social stimuli** – Family, love, community, team, being with people, communicating etc.

Cluster 10    **Basic stimuli** – Survival, health, food, sex, activity etc.

Cluster 11    **Emotional stimuli** – Feelings, passions, drives, desires etc.

Cluster 12    **Demand stimuli** – Orders, instructions, commands, threats, requests etc.

Cluster 13    **Environmental stimuli** – Décor, furniture, light, sound, space, atmosphere, climate etc.

Cluster 14    **Freedom stimuli** – Choice, risk, personal decision making.

Cluster 15    **Negative stimuli** – Set-back, failure, criticism, problems.

Cluster 16    **Change stimuli** – Out of routine, new job, travel, new challenge, new people.

Cluster 17    **Spiritual stimuli** – Understanding and expression of self, principles, beliefs, values etc.

As you review these motivational stimuli and establish a profile of your own motivation, link them to the main areas of motivation, as in the example in Fig. 5.4. When you have determined your own profile and the type of stimuli required to motivate you it is then possible to review whether or not you would like the profile to change and the stimuli needed for this.

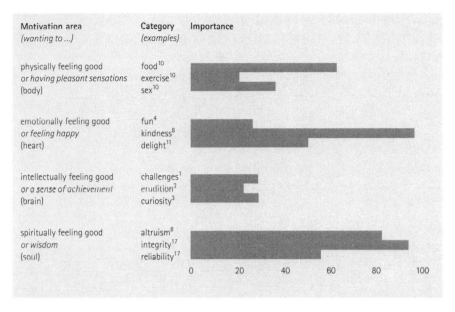

| Motivation area (wanting to ...) | Category (examples) | Importance |
|---|---|---|
| physically feeling good or having pleasant sensations (body) | food[10] exercise[10] sex[10] | |
| emotionally feeling good or feeling happy (heart) | fun[4] kindness[8] delight[11] | |
| intellectually feeling good or a sense of achievement (brain) | challenges[1] erudition[2] curiosity[3] | |
| spiritually feeling good or wisdom (soul) | altruism[8] integrity[17] reliability[17] | |

**Note:** Superscript numerals refer to the appropriate cluster of motivational stimuli

### Fig 5.4
Psychogenetic motivation profile

To reinforce or change your profile of motivation, in order to become a stimulated self, you will then need to expose yourself daily to fresh stimuli. This is the next step.

## 2 Push back the boundaries: expose yourself to fresh stimuli daily

Most of us have a tendency to close our minds down by relying on routines and existing patterns of thought. Without realizing it, we develop habits which degenerate into complacent and unchallenged thinking. As a result we block out new ideas and only see what we are accustomed to seeing. In this way we draw boundaries around our minds and place severe limitations on our experiences of life.

> It is important to go out of our way to expose ourselves to fresh stimuli every single day of our lives

To prevent this it is important to go out of our way to expose ourselves to fresh stimuli every single day of our lives, to discover new ideas and to see things from different perspectives. In this way we can push back the boundaries of our thinking and become a stimulated self. By exposing ourselves to fresh stimuli we can maximize the probability that the occasional stimulus will spark some new thinking, new feelings and new spirit and move us in the desired direction . This cannot happen by default and will only occur if we deliberately seek out fresh stimuli. Here are some potential sources of fresh stimuli:

- different radio programs
- new journals
- different newspapers
- new environment
- travel to new destinations
- new customers
- new music
- new challenges
- questions
- study
- different TV programs
- new films
- new advertisements
- new shops
- new people
- new suppliers
- news
- new projects
- fresh conversation
- crises
- new computing
- new books
- new art
- new theater plays
- new jobs
- competition

- change
- new training
- new work
- unexpected events.

Each of these can be linked to one of the clusters of motivational stimuli, for example:

▶ different radio programs (clusters 2 and 3 – learning and discovery);

▶ new films (cluster 4 – diversionary);

▶ travel to new destinations (clusters 3 and 16 – discovery and change);

▶ new challenges (cluster 1 – aspiration).

By following this process you can seek out the stimuli which spark your motivation and help you become a stimulated self.

Even so, it is unpredictable as to which stimulus will create the desired effect (of stimulating your motivation, your thinking, your feelings, your spirit and therefore your self). In fact most of the new stimuli you expose yourself to will have no effect upon you at all. You will therefore need to experiment with as wide a range of stimuli as possible. This means resisting the temptation to block out new stimuli (or new experiences) and taking the initiative to seek such experience.

What is predictable is the following:

▶ the greater the number of fresh stimuli to which we expose ourselves, the greater the probability that there will be one that reaches our hearts, minds or spirits and sparks an improvement to our own personal approach;

▶ the more we resist exposure to fresh stimuli, the greater the probability that our performance will deteriorate.

Given the excessive bombardment of stimuli that is already trying to target us, this does mean that we have to review the "blocking out – letting in" dynamics of our daily behavior. The regular stimuli of our lives will tend to deaden our senses and drive us into mind-numbing routines. We therefore need to seek out exciting new stimuli which will awaken our senses and help us develop our "selves" (our feelings, our mindsets, our spirits). By exposing ourselves to fresh stimuli we will be able to energize our hearts, challenge our souls and free ourselves of the constraints of the limited learning of the past.

For example, I try to read a different newspaper each day, sometimes two or three. I find that when I buy the same newspaper every day the way I read it becomes routine. My attention follows the same sequencing of news items and articles and my mind slowly becomes attuned to the priorities and thinking of that newspaper. Reading a range of newspapers keeps my mind fresh and helps me detect items that I find stimulating and helpful. This way I am in less danger of having my thinking done for me by the press. I expose myself to different views and opinions and therefore have to form my own judgments rather than rely on those of regular journalists.

Varying the newspapers you read is but one example of how to develop a stimulated self. It draws upon stimuli in the clusters of learning and change. The key is to move out of routine wherever possible. From the list above of potential sources, here are some further practical examples of the way you can open ourselves up to fresh stimuli:

▶ When driving to work use a different route (cluster 16 – change).

▶ Cast your mind back over last week and identify at least one success that occurred and then set yourself the challenge of one success this week (cluster 1 – aspiration).

▶ Tune into different radio channels – listen to talk programs as opposed to music (cluster 2 – learning).

▶ Change the types of books you read, e.g. read history not novels etc. (cluster 7 – inspirational).

▶ Increase your range of entertainment – don't just go to the cinema, go to the theater as well (cluster 4 – diversionary).

▶ Watch different news programs on television (cluster 3 – discovery).

▶ Shop in different places (cluster 16 – change).

▶ Try to identify new things in your environment – i.e. look at things differently (cluster 13 – environmental).

▶ Change your environment – e.g. move furniture around, redecorate etc. (cluster 13 – environmental).

▶ Seek out an opportunity to do something for someone else, whether it is for a beggar in the street or for a colleague in need of help (cluster 8 – altruistic).

▶ Refer to one thought-provoking paragraph in the most important book in your life, the one that embraces the guiding principles in which you believe

– it could be the Bible, the Koran, the Dhammapada, the Talmud or even a book on management that has really influenced you – and then challenge your own behavior in relation to the principle stated in that paragraph (cluster 17 – spiritual).

▶ Try to meet new people as often as possible (cluster 9 – social).

▶ Try to learn something new about the people you already know (clusters 2 and 3 – learning and discovery).

To help you with this list, work out the sources you currently use to stimulate your thinking and then gradually make changes (*see* Table 5.2).

**Table 5.2**

**Changing stimulus sources**

| Current stimulus source (comfort zone) | Change to | New stimulus source (pushing back the boundaries) |
| --- | --- | --- |
| Radio channel (music) | ▶▶▶▶▶▶▶ | Radio channel (talk)[2] |
| Read commentator A in newspaper X | ▶▶▶▶▶▶▶ | Read commentator B in newspaper Y[3] |
| Weekly visit to cinema | ▶▶▶▶▶▶▶ | Occasional theater visit[4] |
| Read novel | ▶▶▶▶▶▶▶ | Read autobiography[7] |
| In-house training | ▶▶▶▶▶▶▶ | External training[2] |
| Internal meetings rooms | ▶▶▶▶▶▶▶ | External venues for meetings[13] |
| Chatting to people you know | ▶▶▶▶▶▶▶ | Chatting to people you don't know[3] |
| Lunching with colleagues | ▶▶▶▶▶▶▶ | Lunching with other teams[9] |
| Frequent visits to X,Y,Z | ▶▶▶▶▶▶▶ | Visit locations rarely visited[16] |
| Having the answers (internal knowledge) | ▶▶▶▶▶▶▶ | Asking questions (lack of knowledge)[3] |

**Note:** Superscript numerals refer to the appropriate cluster of motivational stimuli.

Whenever a fresh stimulus triggers a new thought process, make a note of what happens. It might be a quote from what someone says, or a certain image that evokes a response, or a section of a song that that particularly appeals to you. Try to learn from what is happening to you and discover why this stimulus is having an impact on you. Learning from this can help when it comes to stimulating other people and building relationships with them.

I tend to tear out newspaper articles which spark my interest and regularly make notes in margins of books, sometimes highlighting certain sentences which ring bells with me. All the time I ask myself: what is it about this new stimulus that causes this response inside me? Why does this quote appeal to me? For example, when Ralph Waldo Emerson (1841) writes: "To believe your own thought, to believe that what is true for you in your private heart is true for all men – that is genius," I ask myself, what is the appeal of this statement to me? What can I learn from it? If I hear a piece of music which strikes an emotional chord inside me I try to find out why. Why is that I find Billie Holiday singing the blues so emotionally stimulating? "Strange fruit!" "Fine and mellow!"

## 3 Go out of your way to be stimulated by the people you encounter every day

The third practice for developing a stimulated self is to go out of your way to be stimulated by the people you encounter every day. In practice this means exposing yourself to an increasing number of people and opening yourself up to their ideas.

The harsh reality of life is that there are only a minority of people whose company we really enjoy, whom we find interesting and with whom we want to spend time. These tend to be family members, friends, certain colleagues at work, as well as a small number of business acquaintances and external experts. Regrettably, we do not want to be with the vast majority of people. We avoid most people and tend to be indifferent towards them. This often applies to customers and definitely applies to the vast majority of strangers who cross our paths.

As illustrated in the two boundary diagrams (Figs 5.1 and 5.2) earlier, we accept only a limited number people into the personal space bounded by our emotions and thoughts. These tend to be the people we like and respect and whose own behaviors and communications stimulate our sense of well-being and personal interest. They tend to be

> The more people we expose ourselves to and accept into our hearts and minds, the more stimulating we become

our families, our friends and our colleagues at work. The challenge for us is to push back the boundaries and risk allowing an increasing number of people to come inside our "personal space" and stimulate our emotions and thoughts. People with a narrow circle of friends and acquaintances tend to be boring (if not opinionated), whilst those with a broad band of confidants and acquaintances tend to be much more stimulating. People stimulate each other, therefore the more people we expose ourselves to and accept into our hearts and minds, the more stimulating we become.

This means taking a genuine interest in as many people as physically possible and learning from them. It means allowing ourselves to be influenced and guided by the people we encounter in our everyday lives, whether they be bosses, colleagues or customers. By allowing others to stimulate our hearts and minds, they also will find the relationship stimulating and will therefore be strengthened.

Furthermore, we should go out of our way to locate the experts in our own spheres of interest and then allow them to stimulate our own learning. One of the most stimulating speakers in the world is the guru Tom Peters. During the 1980s I had heard a lot about Tom Peters; I had read his books and seen his videos. But I had never heard him speak live. So on October 18 1991 I went along to a one-day seminar he was giving in London. I was entranced for the whole day. He just blew my mind. I still recall one statement that stimulated me then and stimulates me now. "Dull leaders for dull times. Zany leaders for zany times. If you don't feel crazy, you're not in touch with the times" (Peters, 1992).

For me it was a stimulus to go looking for the unusual, the crazy, the zany, the outrageous. If you go looking for convention you will find the norm – and then you will conform. Given that most of us struggle to sustain our unique identity in the face of the norm, the secret is to seek out that unique identity in others and allow it to stimulate the development of our own.

Here are some practical examples of the way you can go out of your way to be stimulated by others:

▶ When entering a room full of people go out of your way to talk to the strangers, not just your friends.

▶ When walking through an office greet everyone and try to strike up conversations with people you don't know.

▶ Try to learn something new about every person you encounter.

▶ Find out what turns people on.

▶ Seek out people who are stimulating and spend time with them.

▶ Take a genuine interest in everyone you meet.

▶ Go out of your way to meet one interesting new person every day.

▶ Seize every opportunity to meet the experts and learn from them.

When you drive home in the evening challenge yourself to answer this question: "Who did I meet today who was stimulating – and what was so stimulating about them?" Set yourself a target to be stimulated by at least new person every day. You will be amazed how exciting life becomes when you go out of your way to do this. All it means is that you have to start to chatting to people you don't normally chat to. Today it was the optician who gave me an eye test. It was not just her thoroughness, professionalism and expertise in conducting the test that appealed to me but her personal approach. I was absolutely convinced that she loved her work and was doing her absolute best for me. Striving for the best on every occasion is a rare quality – she had it and I found it incredibly stimulating.

## 4 Create at work, one "work of art" at least once a month, ideally once a week

Creating a "work of art" at work again relates to the principle of going beyond the immediate task in hand and stimulating yourself to add something special to whatever you are doing.

A little while back I was hired in by a government agency to run a series of one-day management seminars around the UK. This meant travelling by plane or train to some very distant parts of the country. As I had a computer to take with me, together with an overnight change of clothes, I was very limited as to what additional baggage I could carry. It was just not possible to take all the seminar documentation with me – it would have been too heavy. I therefore mailed ahead of me a master of the handouts I would be using, so that the administrator at each location could produce sufficient copies for distribution to the large number of delegates attending each seminar. The interesting thing was this. At most locations the administrator merely photocopied the handouts on to white paper and stapled them together, exactly as requested. One location was different however. The administrator there was very special and made the production of each handout a work of art. She copied the handouts on to tinted paper, produced a special cover with a graphic design and then had each delegate's name neatly typed onto it. Finally, she carefully bound each copy. She had turned my master handout into a beautiful work of art, whereas everyone else had merely photo-copied it on to white paper and stapled it. Not surprisingly it was this location that excelled in most aspects of performance.

> Every task you undertake is an opportunity to convert a routine job into a work of art

Every task you undertake is an opportunity to convert a routine job into a work of art. The limitation, of course, is time – it would be impossible to invest sufficient time to produce continuous works of art. However, this should not stop you from aiming to produce at least one work of art every month, or ideally every week.

It is art that stimulates. People love creativity and that is why we visit art galleries, go to concerts, see brilliant films and read great novels. By pure coincidence whilst writing this I am listening to Miles Davis's recording of "It never entered my mind." It may never have entered your mind to produce art at work, possibly because you have a limited definition of art in your mind. If you extend the definition to something that is creative, special and stimulates others, then you will find innumerable opportunities to produce "works of art" at work. How you serve coffee can be a work of art. On my visits to various companies I have been served coffee in a hundred different ways, only one or two of which appeal. Why not add value to the visitor's experience by making the act of serving coffee an artistic performance? In the Far East serving tea to a guest is a fine art form.

Art is not easy and you will need frequent practice and constant endeavor to improve your approach. However, the more you apply yourself the more skilled you will become and the more others will be stimulated by your creativity and feel special as a result.

Here are some practical examples of "works of art" you can aim to produce at work:

▹ Turn the way you greet visitors to your office into a work of art (make it special, not routine).

▹ Turn your next meeting into a work of art (make it different from the last meeting).

▹ Ensure your next presentation is a work of art (don't rely on the same old bullet points and standard background).

▹ Prepare your next report as a work of art (it's not just what you write but how you write and present it).

▹ Organize your next training session as a work of art (do something unconventional and creative).

▹ Turn your desk into a work of art (turn it into a visually stunning exhibit that excites the interest of passers-by whilst keeping you stimulated).

▹ Decorate your office as a work of art (make a trip through your office a fascinating experience).

By creating works of art at work you will convert the mundane into something exceptionally special which will set you apart from the rest. Whilst there is no guarantee that any one work of art will have an impact, there is a guarantee that the more you work at your art the greater the probability that your unique contribution will be recognized and appreciated – by customers and colleagues alike.

## 5 Always have at least one learning challenge

To become a stimulated self it is critical that you learn something new every day of your life.

Learning comes in two forms:

- by accident
- by design.

Learning by accident just happens to us. We go through an experience and emerge with some incidental learning that we have absorbed in readiness for the next time we have that experience. For example, we might be working at the computer screen when a colleague approaches and starts chatting about the task in hand. The colleague might then point out that there is a short-cut we could use to speed up the task. We learn and in future always use that particular short-cut.

Learning by design is different. We set ourselves a personal goal to acquire some new knowledge or skill and then go out of our way to develop that knowledge or skill. We seek out the appropriate training courses from which we can benefit, we search for the books and journals that we can study and that will bring us the requisite expertise, and we hunt down the top experts in the field from whom we can learn. For example, we might set ourselves the goal of becoming exceptionally knowledgeable and skilled in the use of PowerPoint Presentations so that we become expert not only in all the techniques of animation, online broadcasting, video and audio inserts but also in developing designs that have a powerful visual impact and that maximize the stimulus of the message we wish to impart.

People who wish to become a stimulated self are always learning and will always have at least one current learning challenge facing them. As soon as they acquire a fairly high degree of expertise in the given area they will then set themselves a fresh learning challenge. These people tend to be self-critical, self-effacing, curious, hard-working, as well as eager to learn. They seem to have this constant drive to improve themselves, to add increasingly to their repertoire of skills, knowledge, experience and expertise, and to add value to whatever they do.

This thirst for knowledge, this desperate desire to improve, this constant curiosity is a rare quality and tends to be exhibited by the more successful people in life. They are stimulated by learning and in themselves thus become stimulating. They ask questions all the time and are never satisfied, because they know they will never have all the answers.

More frequently I come across people who are passive, who have not set themselves learning goals (whatever their job), who delude themselves they know it all and have little to learn, who are not prepared to work hard and not aware they need to apply themselves in a process of self-improvement. Frequently I run seminars with a room full of people who are there only because their bosses told them to attend and because they see an opportunity to escape the monotony of their everyday routine. They expect to be entertained and have the trainer spoon-feed them with brilliant ideas that will transform them into they know not what. To quote Daniel Goleman (1998):

> Estimates of the extent to which skills taught in company training programs carrying over into day to day practice on the job are as low – and gloomy – as a mere 10 percent. But no one knows for sure ... because the data are rarely collected.

Here is a suggested learning challenge for today:

- Identify one person you know who is incredibly stimulating.
- Identify another who fails to stimulate you.
- List out the detailed qualities, characteristics, attributes, behaviors that differentiate the two and then relate yourself to them.
- How would most people classify you?
- What have you learnt and what action can you take as a result?

A further challenge for tomorrow is to set yourself a long-term learning challenge in order to develop your own expertise and thus enable you to become even more stimulating as a person.

## 6 Use personal aspiration as a key stimulus

The soporific effect of contentment, satisfaction, comfort and security rapidly leads to complacency and decay. Stasis is a fleeting illusion, whilst stimulus regression is both a reality and threat when we fail to aspire to improvement. In other words, throughout life and especially at work we constantly have to strive for improvement. There is no stopping-off point when we can comfortably say "We've made it, we're there, we're okay now, we needn't bother any more, we know how."

In 1982 when I was on the board of the airline British Caledonian the largest transatlantic carrier was PanAm. Can you fly from Heathrow to New York on PanAm today? As a teenager I used to hang out with my mates at Wimpey Bars. At that point in time we had never heard of McDonald's or BurgerKing. Where are Wimpy Bars today? Like PanAm they are still around, but not to the extent they were a couple of decades ago. Furthermore, where are the brands of beer we used to drink of old? In those days we had certainly not heard of Budweiser or the brands people drink today. Nor had we heard of Virgin, Starbucks, Borders or Office Depot.

> Throughout life and especially at work we constantly have to strive for improvement

Our success as individuals is the product of our personal aspirations. Without aspiration we resign ourselves to a life driven by forces external to ourselves. Destiny will control us unless we aspire to control our own destiny.

Therefore the most powerful stimulus in becoming a stimulated self is personal aspiration. The origin of personal aspiration, whilst it might be prompted and inspired by external factors, lies in the depths of our soul and evolves from the exciting process of self-discovery and an awareness of "What I am all about in life and what I want to be." As Brian Tracy (1998) writes: "Everything and anything I ever accomplish in life is up to me. I am completely responsible. No one is going to do it for me."

Whilst at times we might be driven by events and benefit from luck (being in the right place at the right time), it is aspiration that helps us seize upon the chances that life constantly creates for us. It is through aspiration that we recognize the opportunities that daily cross our paths. In fact, some would argue that it is through aspiration we create the necessary opportunities. Thus if we aspire to having a book published we will in all probability create opportunities to meet people who can guide us in this direction.

For decades now the standard textbooks on management have stressed the importance of individual goal setting and measuring performance objectively against the accomplishment of these goals. Regrettably, this is not always effective, for the simple reason that often there is a lack of convergence between company-imposed goals and individual aspirations. People are assigned budgets they struggle to live with, are set targets they believe impossible to achieve and then play games to massage the figures to convince the powers-that-be that everything is on track. Such "systems" of goal setting frequently fail to stimulate and inspire and normally tend towards a process of manipulation and pretence.

Aspiration is personal and is driven by the essence of what we are about individually as human beings. It relates to what *we* want to achieve, as opposed to what *they* want to achieve – although ideally the two should merge. It relates to the minutiae of our behavior on a minute-to-minute basis, as well as to our longer term ambitions in life. It relates to what we wish to achieve when answering an unsolicited call at 10.30 am on a Thursday morning, but also to what we intend as our personal accomplishments at the year end.

Our aspirations reflect what we want of ourselves at any particular moment in the future, whether it be at the end of the next meeting or the end of the next quarter. The more focused we are on our aspirations, the more stimulated we will become in determining the actions necessary to accomplish them.

Here are some practical examples of personal aspirations:

- "I want our team to be the first in the company to receive more compliments than complaints from customers in any given month."

- "I want our team to be so incredibly motivated that no one leaves for negative reasons."

- "I want people queuing up to join our team."

- "At least once a month we will do something for our customers that is special and which they will really appreciate."

- "I want every single member of the team to benefit from the very best training that is available, to help them make further progress."

- "Every day we will have a reason to celebrate some success."

- "Our team will be seen as a school for promotion in the company."

- "I will develop my personal presentation skills such that everyone is asking for me to give presentations."

Your challenge today, in becoming a stimulated self, is to find some time to reflect upon what you are really all about as a person at work. What really drives you? What are you really seeking to achieve? Deep down what are your innermost aspirations?

If you can identify and focus on these, then in all probability you will develop a powerfuls stimulus to achieve them. Everything is possible.

## 7 Let your true self shine through

"If work is all about *doing* then the soul is all about *being*" wrote David Whyte (1994). To put the stimulus factor to work it is critical not only to consider what you "do" at work but also what you "are" there.

This means trying to allow your true self to shine through in as much of your behavior and communication at work as possible – a task which most people find incredibly difficult as they act out roles and conform to conventions to which they don't necessarily subscribe. Ideally everything you do must be a reflection of your true self. You should try to allow your genuine nature to emerge in your various

> Try to allow your genuine nature to emerge in your various dealings with colleagues and customers

dealings with colleagues and customers, as well as in everything you say – whether at meetings, in presentations, in reports or informally in conversation.

Regrettably and mostly inadvertently we allow the original and intended purity of our souls to become corrupted with impurities. This normally takes the form of negative thinking, as evidenced by grudges, grievances, prejudices, bad feelings, suppression, denial (of the obvious), anger, irritation, intolerance and many other aspects we see in people's daily behavior. These we need to sweep away to allow our true selves to shine through. By allowing our negativity to show we are not being true to the humble purity of our own souls, but more to a distorted and exaggerated image of ourself.

Life is not that perfect that we can avoid things going wrong, people doing things we dislike and generally things not going our way from time to time. Throughout life everyone faces difficulties and our tendency is to blame others for them. As a result, we tend to develop a highly sanitized perception of ourselves, whilst attributing all the wrongs of the world to other people. In doing so, we tarnish our souls with negativity. We lose sight of ourselves for what we really are, projecting ourselves as icons of rationality whilst slating others for their unreasonable behavior. The popular press is full of such irrational projections ("If only the politicians did it our way!").

We are humble souls struggling as much as any other for the right way forward. By allowing clouds of negativity to hide our souls we lose sight of our true selves and thus allow our relationships with other imperfect beings to become corrupted with bad feelings. When we do allow glimmers of our true good nature to shine through people find it exceptionally stimulating.

Everything in life accumulates grime and therefore anything of use needs to be cleaned periodically in order to remove the grime. For example, we frequently need to take a shower, shampoo our hair, wash our clothes, clean the windows and sweep the floor to remove grime. We need to do the same to the windows of our souls. The negativity that we daily acquire is equivalent to layers of grime building up to obscure our minds, hearts and souls in the way we think and feel. This grime of emotional negativity and irrationality distorts perceptions, leads to unpleasant behaviors and corrupts our relationships with others. Our challenge therefore is methodically to cleanse the window on our souls and hearts, to purify our thinking and feelings and to eliminate the negativity. In this way we can rediscover the very goodness of our own natures and be in a better position to relate to others.

The stimulated self is one in which the true good self emerges and stimulates others with ideas underpinned by openness, honesty and integrity. Conversely, the selfish self is one in which the prime driving force is self-interest and personal acquisition. In other words, in putting the stimulus factor to work in becoming a stimulated self there is substantial ethical dimension.

Here are some practical examples of how you might let your true self shine through:

- Show genuine enthusiasm – don't simulate it.
- Only speak the truth, but be careful in the way you speak your mind.
- In speaking your mind, always seek to be constructive, never destructive.
- Let your feelings show, but first eliminate all negative feelings.
- Always aim to help the people you are with (whoever they are) – never try to make them feel bad.
- Act and communicate in accordance with your own beliefs, not those of others.
- Develop a passion for the most stimulating aspects of your work and let this passion show through to others.

▶ Only say "No" as a last resort.

▶ Don't seek to impress but allow others to impress you.

▶ Always give other people the benefit of the doubt.

▶ Never give yourself the benefit of the doubt – always choose what you believe is right.

▶ Never hide your ignorance, except when others might exploit it.

▶ Conversely, only lend your expertise to people you trust.

▶ Trust everyone except those who have let you down in a bad way.

▶ Try to forgive and forget, but don't kill yourself in the process.

▶ Putting people first means never putting yourself first.

▶ Challenge yourself all the time: your thoughts, your feelings, your opinions, your values and beliefs, your judgments and the minutiae of your own behavior and communications.

## 8 Talk to yourself in a challenging but constructive way

It is essential that virtually on a daily basis you create space to reflect. You will need to find a far corner of your physical environment where you can access the far corners of your mind, heart and soul. You will need to free yourself of interruption and then seize this opportunity to ask yourself many questions.

Here are some space-creating opportunities:

▶ Go for a long walk most days.

▶ Go for a swim in the local pool.

▶ Go and sit in a café where none of your colleagues will find you.

▶ Take a bus, train or plane to somewhere and just reflect on the questions below.

Equally important as daily reflection is the need for occasional long weekends away from your normal routines, as well as the traditional two-week vacations in distant parts. All provide essential opportunities to reflect and recharge your energies using some fresh stimuli.

Here are the sorts of questions you should be asking yourself regularly:

▶ Why am I doing this job?

▶ What do I feel passionate about in my life and in my work?

▶ What are the long-term aspirations in my life?

▶ What are the short-term aspirations I have every day when I go to work?

▶ What have I learnt recently?

▶ Do I really know what other people think of me? Am I brave enough to find out?

▶ Do I really know my weaknesses and do I genuinely admit my mistakes?

▶ Am I as honest with myself as I like to make out?

▶ Do I really try to do my best for others?

▶ Do I genuinely try to learn from others?

▶ Do I reach out to others or do I close myself in from them?

▶ Am I selfish? Am I arrogant? Am I inconsiderate? Do I listen with genuine interest to what others say? Am I narrow-minded? Am I humble?

▶ Am I any good?

▶ Am I "me"? Or do I try to act as if I was someone else?

▶ What am I all about in life?

These are simple but profound questions that will stimulate your mind, heart and soul – that's if you are prepared to put them to your "self." The most important criterion is that you be must scrupulously honest with yourself in answering these questions. If you gloss over them or attempt to fob yourself off with platitudes or deceptions then you are destined to disillusion everyone you know as well as yourself.

In summary by taking the eight practical steps above you will be able to develop into a stimulated self and become a stimulating person to whom other people will want to relate.

# 6

# The stimulus
# of leadership

I see my role as a provider. I am a team player. It is what I can
do for the team. I want to help each team player to be
successful in accomplishing their successes. My role is to provide
the tools and resources. I don't have all the answers. I get the
team together to find the answers. I believe that people want to
do the right thing. It's believing in your team and what they
accomplish. I let them take risks and it's okay if they
occasionally fall down. My motivation comes from watching
other people be successful. It's my sole motivation. It's watching
each team member accomplish their personal and professional
goals. That's all I need, then I'm juiced.
*Gerry Busk, Senior Vice-President, Consumer Banking,*
*BankAtlantic, USA*

## The leader, the manager and the boss

There is an ongoing debate about the difference between a manager and a
leader. Dr John Viney (2000) argues that "management qualifies as a
science" and relates to "analysis, logical processes, systems, planning,
problem solving, rationality and detail" whereas "leadership is centered
around personality" and relates to "charisma, vision, strategies, motivation
of people, dreams, drive and originality."

In other words, according to Dr Viney it is leaders who attempt to
motivate people whilst it is managers are primarily concerned with processes

and systems. In my view the two are inextricably linked. The issue is more of semantics than of differentiated roles. Any person who has responsibilities for a team of people can be called a manager or leader depending on the language and culture of the organization. The role of such a manager or a leader will embrace both the personal and impersonal sides of ensuring that an assigned team of people achieve specified results. The personal side relates to motivation whilst the impersonal side relates to processes and systems. In fact I would argue that the prime role of a leader or manager relates to helping a team of people achieve specified goals and thus supporting them in a variety of ways, including the provision of effective administrative processes and support systems. I have yet to come across a manager of a team who is not meant to lead them.

Overall I prefer to use the idiomatic term "boss" to refer to a leader or manager. People do not say "I'm going to see my leader." Sometimes they say "I'm going to see my manager," although this tends to have a formal ring about it. More often they say "I'm going to see the boss." However I will use all three terms throughout this chapter.

## The orchestration of stimuli

The motivation of a boss (or leader or manager) and a team to achieve a specified set of goals is inextricably linked to the stimulus of aspiration. The greater the convergence between "work" aspirations of individual team members, the leader and the company, the higher the motivation and the probability of high performance.

One of the central theses of this book is that managers (or leaders or bosses) cannot motivate their employees directly, for the simple reason that all motivation is self-motivation. At best, leaders can attempt to stimulate the motivation of their people by drawing from one or more of the 17 clusters of stimuli mentioned previously. The prime role of a leader is therefore to orchestrate these stimuli so that people are energized or motivated to respond by giving the best performance possible. The leader generates a range of external stimuli that maximizes the possibility of internally stimulating the motivation of the people he or she leads. The range of external stimuli that have the potential to motivate people, whilst grouped here into

> The prime role of a leader is to orchestrate stimuli so that people are motivated to respond by giving the best performance possible

17 clusters, is vast. It therefore requires a considerable amount of experi-mentation along with experience to determine which set of external stimuli is most likely to generate the internal stimuli necessary for motivating any one individual or team. Learning from experimentation (with personal behavior) and from experience (of the impact of such personal behavior) is thus essential to developing the leadership necessary to stimulate motivation and effect high performance.

When experimenting with various motivational stimuli it is worth focusing initially on seven clusters from which a leader can draw. These are:

- **Aspirational stimuli** – Agreeing with each individual and the team a challenge they want to achieve.

- **Freedom stimuli** – Allowing people to get on and do their jobs, allowing them to make the appropriate decisions and giving them scope to take initiatives and be creative.

- **Personal value stimuli** – Demonstrating that employees are genuinely valued and appreciated and that their individual unique contributions are recognized.

- **Learning stimuli** – Creating opportunities for people to enhance their own value with improved skills and knowledge.

- **Emotional stimuli** – Generating positive feelings throughout.

- **Change stimuli** – Alleviating the boredom and monotony of the same old routines by introducing variation and change to the patterns of work.

- **Spiritual stimuli** – Using personally held principles, beliefs and values as a basis for all behaviors and decisions.

Table 6.1 gives more specific examples of how a leader can draw from the various clusters of stimuli and use them to stimulate the motivation of an individual or team. These examples are not intended as a prescription but serve to illustrate the application of motiva-tional stimuli.

A motivated team of people is one that is stimulated

A motivated team of people is one that is stimulated. As Table 6.1 illus-trates, the stimuli can come from any one or more of the 17 clusters. The opportunity to stimulate members of the team comes with virtually every interaction with them, either individually or collectively, and requires the conscious creation of a spark of positive emotional, intellectual or spiritual energy which will ignite their energies. However, too much stimulation will

## Table 6.1

### Stimulating the motivation of an individual or team

| Cluster | External stimulus (from leader) | Internal stimulus (from employee/team) |
|---|---|---|
| 1 Aspirational | We have an exciting new challenge. | I want to rise to this, it will give me some incredibly valuable experience. |
| 2 Learning | We need to learn about XYZ. | This really interests me. |
| 3 Discovery | It's essential we find out about this market segment. | I'd loved to be involved with this. |
| 4 Diversionary | I'd like to spend five minutes running a product knowledge quiz. | This will be great fun. |
| 5 Reward | There's a $50 voucher for everyone who achieves target today. | It's the icing on the cake – I'll go for it. |
| 6 Personal value | Thanks for all your efforts in completing that urgent project. | I'am glad my efforts are recognized and appreciated. |
| 7 Inspirational | What Kacey Smith did was really creative. We need some more great ideas like that. | The story about Kacey is inspirational. I have a brilliant idea I want to pursue too. |
| 8 Altruistic | Department B are really up against it – we need to put in some extra time to help them. | I'd be happy to help out. |
| 9 Social | I'm organizing an informal lunch time session this Friday to get up-to-date with each other. | I'm really looking forward to this. |
| 10 Basic/physical | I'm arranging a voluntary program of callisthenics at 3.00 pm every day. | I can stretch my body as well as my mind. |
| 11 Emotional | I really feel strongly about ... | I don't want the boss to feel bad about this – I'd better do something about it. |
| 12 Demand | I'm afraid I have to insist on this. | You're the boss – I'll accept your decision. |
| 13 Environmental | I'll support any initiative you take to improve the office décor. | Here's a chance to brighten up our surroundings. We'll take this on and talk to building services about it. |
| 14 Freedom | The budget's yours – you must decide. | There are some exciting options we must explore. |
| 15 Negative | Losing this contract is a major blow. | We'll try harder next time. |
| 16 Change | We need to get away for an off-site meeting. | The break will do us good. |
| 17 Spiritual | I believe this is an issue of principle and fundamental to the way we operate. | The boss is right – we cannot behave this way towards a customer. |

result in satiation or a dulling of the senses. As mentioned in a previous chapter, the effect of a specific motivation stimulus can wear off if too frequently used.

## Creating fresh positive stimuli

Many of the external stimuli managers produce are not created consciously but are products of ingrained behaviors driven by subconscious internal stimuli. Managers just do things without thinking. The end result is a pattern of stale habits comprising routine behaviors and the repetition of the same old uninspired ways of communicating. This can have a reciprocal effect on staff as they retreat into their shells and follow their own frayed routines. When this happens, thought processes become automatic and essential stimuli that might spark a fresh train of thought are blocked out. By blocking out such stimuli the ability to generate fresh stimuli to spark the motivation of our teams is restricted.

The subconscious stimuli that generate automatic behaviors cannot be assigned to any one of the clusters, since there is no conscious process involved. In other words, we do things that affect other people without being aware of the impact we are having. One of the keys to this is to break through the barriers of routine and habit and open ourselves up to fresh external stimuli so that we can, in turn, energize jaded staff.

Here are just a few examples, drawn from the responses of the hundreds of people I interviewed, of management behaviors that can stimulate either a positive or negative response from team members, depending on the existing levels of motivation. The examples are in alphabetical order of the person speaking.

### David Askwith

Art Director, Saatchi and Saatchi, UK

I believe a boss can help motivate. When you've been working for six months with no holiday and you've only got two bits of work out (say the client is being difficult) then the boss can keep you going with his optimism.

The stimulus here is the boss's "optimism," which derives from the clusters of aspirational and emotional stimuli.

## Sir Richard Branson

Chairman, Virgin Group, UK

I like to enable other people to challenge themselves in the same way as I challenge myself.

The stimulus here is "enabling people to challenge themselves." "Enabling" relates to the stimulus of freedom whilst "challenge" relates to aspiration.

## Jean Carvalho

Executive Vice-President, BankAtlantic, USA

Normally I know what my boss Alan Levan (the President) wants to achieve. His expectations of me are extremely high. He tells me that. We sit together four times a year to review progress. I inform him of things I have done. I will ask him if he thinks I am going in the right direction. He will say "You are doing great, but let's talk about this, I'm not sure how much mileage we got out of it." He has the ability to pull the best out of me. I go away from meetings with him feeling highly charged. He'll tell me we've got a problem, say on the West Coast, and he'll ask me to go and fix it. And I will. He will say "I know I came to the right person" when it's fixed. He's quick to encourage and support. He makes me feel that there's nothing I touch that I don't turn to magic. Therefore I have no option but to turn it to magic. I have to make magic for him.

The stimuli here relate to aspirations ("expectations") and personal value ("you are doing great") as well as emotion ("I go away feeling highly charged") and inspiration ("magic").

## Dr Liz Clark

Hepatitis Product Manager, Schering-Plough, UK

My boss Brian increased my bonus. What made it motivational was that he took the action. It wasn't the money itself. What demotivates me is not being appreciated. It's when people don't say thank you. Years ago with a previous boss we worked on a project where everyone pulled out all the stops and we achieved what had to be achieved. No one said "thank you." It wasn't appreciated.

The stimulus here relates to personal value. It was the action Brian took that stimulated the sense of personal value. In the second instance it was the lack of such a stimulus.

## Helen Downey

Service Excellence Manager, Virgin Trains, UK

What motivates me is challenge. Something that you can't wait to get your teeth into and when you get near (to achieving it) you say "wow." I try to set myself challenges. If I don't have a challenge each day I get bored, I get itchy. Challenge is a daily thing. I have to keep active. I set myself a goal every morning I have to achieve. I tend to go from one extreme to another. If things are too easy I get demotivated. I've had bosses who set goals which are not clear. Then I get frustrated perhaps demotivated. Perhaps it's because of my hurry-up drive. As long I have a set of clear goals I'm happy.

The stimulus here relates to aspiration. When goals are not clear aspirations disappear, with the resulting risk of demotivation.

## Elise

Worker at a tourist attraction, Singapore

When they do say "thank you" it's like a rehearsed script. It's not genuine. The words are not spoken from the heart. The managers are insincere. There's no unity amongst the workers.

What are lacking here are the emotional and spiritual stimuli. The managers are going through the motions without the essential stimuli that their hearts and souls should provide.

## Lina

Hotel cleaner, Singapore

I've only been here for five months. It's a very friendly hotel. The bosses are friendly, the people I work with are friendly and I think the customers are friendly too. My previous hotel wasn't like that. Nobody bothered.

The key stimulus to motivation here is social. People are stimulated by friendly behaviors, whether they be from bosses, colleagues or customers.

## Richard Killoran

General Manager, Austin Reed, Piccadilly Store, London, UK

I'm totally self-motivated. I'm a self-starter. Even so, Roger Jennings, our Managing Director, motivates me. He has energy, drive and vision. He is always very positive. You rub against him for 30 seconds and he energizes you. He has charisma. I know when I'm doing a good job. But I do like to be told.

Here the stimuli are clearly emotional and aspirational. The motivational energies of the Managing Director stimulate the energies of the other person.

## Kate Ogunbanke

Customer Care Assistant, Virgin Trains, UK

In here it's like a family. There are seven of us. It's teamwork. It's a wonderful company to work for and I'm happy. I can't wait to get to work. I love my job. Liz McDonald is a wonderful boss. She treats you like a human being, she puts you at ease. She comes to your level, makes you feel important. She is encouraging and understanding. She's got the milk of human kindness. I've met Richard Branson. He's very unassuming. He's wonderful. Someone like that you expect to be untouchable, unapproachable. But he mixes with everyone. He's very good.

Three of the key stimuli involved here are social ("family" and "he mixes with everyone"), spiritual (the principle of "treating you like a human being"), as well as personal value ("she makes you feel important").

## Jules Szwarzak

Director, London North-East Region, NatWest Bank, UK

The job I've had for the last two-and-a-half years is the best I've ever had. I'm motivated by power, not in a macho, aggressive sense, but the power to influence 2500 people. If 2500 staff go home and feel good (and then make their families feel good) then I've made a difference. I get a buzz when I feel it's happening. It can be electrifying. It's when people are happy. I like the space to do things. I'm not a funny person but I like to have fun at work. I've just been in a very serious meeting, about costs, and we laughed quite a bit.

Four clusters of motivational stimuli are involved here. The first is altruistic ("I want people to be happy"), the second is freedom ("I like the space to do things"), the third is diversionary ("I like to have fun at work") and the fourth is emotional ("I get a buzz").

## George Westwell

General Manager, London Metropole Hilton Hotel

Our Managing Director, Anthony Harris, is very good at motivating people. He has no airs and graces. He calls a spade a spade. Once he came here and he started helping behind the bar. It came naturally to him, he didn't do it for effect. He treats people like human beings. It's not just what he does but the sincerity and trust behind it. He's genuine.

The main stimulus here relates to practising a deeply held set of values and beliefs ("sincerity", "trust" and being "genuine") and thus draws from the spiritual cluster.

## Clare Wheadon

New Policies Adviser, WPA Health Insurance, UK

I find it really motivating working here, building up relationships with customers and making it happen for them – *because of me*. It's a sense of achievement. When something positive happens. I have a success, I say to myself "I want to do that again." My boss is brilliant, fabulous. He's supportive, encouraging. He organizes training for you. You can always go to him. If you do something well here you are told about it. We have a strong social life. We mix a lot out of work. This is very important. We build up strong relationships. You can learn so much more about people outside the workplace and this helps in the workplace.

It is worth highlighting five clusters here. The first relates to aspiration ("sense of achievement"), the second is social ("we have a strong social life"), third relates to personal value ("we are told when we do something well") and the fourth to learning ("training" and "you can learn so much more"). Finally, there is a very powerful emotional stimulus working here ("My boss is brilliant, fabulous. He's supportive, encouraging").

## David Wilmot

Customer Service Manager, The Equitable Life Assurance Society, UK

I am motivated when I receive feedback (praise, congratulations) – this goes miles. I was delighted to have a salary increase recently but it was the words that went with it (from Phil Stone, my boss) that meant much more.

The stimulus cluster here is that of personal value ("the words that went with it meant much more").

# Conscious awareness of behavioral stimuli

One of the lessons that can be drawn from the 13 examples given above is that successful bosses are sensitive to the potential impact their behavior can have on people and how it can stimulate either a positive or negative response. To achieve this, they become increasingly aware of the potential damage certain types of subconscious behavioral stimuli have and thus consciously strive to generate behaviors which act as a positive stimulus in the relationships they have with their teams. At the same time, they strive to eliminate any behaviors that might act as a negative stimulus. This requires creating a conscious awareness of all the stimuli we produce that potentially have a negative or positive impact on other people. This can only be accomplished by allowing our conscious thought processes to intervene, so as to modify behavioral stimuli which had previously been generated automatically through various subconscious processes.

## The minutiae of behavior

It is these minutiae of behavior that can stimulate immense motivational energies in people. Managers who are insensitive to the importance of these nuances risk stimulating negative energies and demotivation. Leading people is thus a fine art and requires orchestrating a wide range of positive stimuli. In the absence of such orchestration there will be no beautiful music but just discordant noise. It is this noise that I hear in many companies as people bellyache about their bosses.

One interviewee in the research told me:

We get out on the road, we achieve our targets, we do our jobs as best we can but we get no feedback from our manager. He just takes it for granted. We don't know if he thinks we're doing a good job or not. The only time he calls us in is when there's a problem, or a complaint, or he needs something extra. We get no praise, no thanks and most of the time we don't really know what's going on. I get on well with my colleagues and that's why I come to work. I love working with these people despite our boss. We all think the same. When we do something special for a customer or receive some positive feedback from one, that really turns us on. We turn each other on. Our customers turn us on. But our boss is on a different planet. He's always in meetings, he doesn't understand what we do, he's not really interested. He doesn't bother. Whenever we see him we just humor him. He did go on a management course once and came back all fired up trying to put this motivational stuff into practice, but it wasn't real and it soon faded and then he reverted to his normal indifferent self. We confronted him once with the way we felt but he became defensive, saying he preferred to let us get on and do our job without too much interference. But the only time we see him is when he interferes because his own bosses want something, or he's had a complaint, or he wants to screw more out of us.

In the above case the manager is inadvertently emitting a discordant set of negative stimuli that have the potential to demotivate his team. Compare this to the following statement from one of the people interviewed:

I think my boss respects and trusts me. What I like about him is that he takes me into his confidence. He'll say "Khalid, I've got a problem and I'd welcome your advice." He's very open with me and I feel I can be open with him too. He never makes you feel bad. In fact it's the reverse. I always feel good with him.

The stimulus here is of personal value. The manager values Khalid and shows it by seeking Khalid's advice. It is this behavior that stimulates the motivation. The other stimulus is emotional. The manager generates positive emotions in Khalid and makes him feel good.

Another example of how a manager's behavior can stimulate a motivational impact on a team relates to my own experience. In an early part of my own management career I was responsible for a team of approximately 20 people. Whilst I thought I was doing everything necessary to motivate my team I didn't realize that they actually hated me and I did not discover this until we went away for a team-building session facilitated by a consultant. At the time I was a "workaholic," getting into the office at 7.30 am every morning and not leaving till after 6.30 pm most evenings. I never put pressure on my team to work the same long hours as me and they normally came in just before 9.00 am and left promptly at 5.30 pm. I ran frequent team sessions but all I ever received was polite contributions and innocuous questions. If ever a team put a report on my desk just before 5.30 pm I would read it that evening and have a response ready for their arrival at 9.00 am the following morning. I thought I was being communicative, decisive and efficient. What I did not realize was that my "workaholic" behavior was stimulating a negative response amongst the team. I was making them feel guilty. They saw me there working hard in the office when they arrived in the morning and the same when they left in the afternoon. Not only did they have guilty feelings, but they perceived I was putting them under pressure because of the way I turned reports around quickly and made decisions. My behavior stimulated bad feelings in the team – they felt they could not please me because their own work rates were lower than mine (although because of their own family responsibilities they were constrained from raising their own work rates to my "workaholic" level).

So they channelled their motivational energies into endless discussions over coffee about "What to do about David." They found solace by crying on each other's shoulders about this impossible boss. The stimulus to their motivation became one of "negative" discovery, to highlight something else David had done which they could then moan about when he was not around. "Do you know what happened today? David came into the office to ask about the recruitment exercise and he didn't even enquire about my weekend and how my mother is – and it was only last Thursday that I told him she had been taken ill."

And on it went. My behavior was stimulating bad feelings amongst my staff and I was totally unaware of it. The motivational energies that I was inadvertently stimulating related to personal criticism (of me), intrigue, gossip and rumor. My team was thriving on this. My behavior, which they perceived as poor, became the focus of their motivational energies. They could not wait to meet at lunch to discover what further demotivational blunders I had committed. Inevitably the more blunders I accidentally committed the more motivated they were to look for them and discover them.

I only became aware of all this when the facilitator flushed out all these feelings at a team session and we were then able to address them. It was a painful experience for me, but a valuable learning exercise.

To develop as a leader one must consciously examine all those behaviors that have previously been driven subconsciously and therefore acted as inadvertent stimuli to others' behavior. Often we cannot see ourselves for what we are. This is one of the biggest challenges facing any leader. Keep asking the question: "How do the people in the team really see me?"

Many bosses are unaware of the impact they are having on their team. They are unaware of the stimuli they are emitting and the responses they therefore generate. When the response is negative, people tend to channel their motivational energies in other directions, for example by trying to get a new job, or working less hard so they can spend more time chatting (or moaning and groaning) with their colleagues, or spending more time at home. I have seen front-line staff reading magazines and ignoring customers, as well as back office people huddled in groups chatting away and neglecting to answer ringing telephones. It is not that these people are demotivated, it is just that they have responded to a negative stimulus from their bosses by channelling their positive motivational energies in a different direction: away from the company and its customers.

> Often we cannot see ourselves for what we are. This is one of the biggest challenges facing any leader. Keep asking the question: "How do the people in the team really see me?"

All motivation is aimed at generating positive feelings and overcoming or moving away from any negative feelings. This applies to everything we do in life. This is why all motivation is self-motivation. When someone makes us feel bad we are self-motivated to minimize or eliminate that feeling by moving in a direction that makes us feel good. That is motivation – it is self-motivation. If our bosses make us feel bad, they are not only inadvertently demotivating us but also effectively motivating us to move in another direction that makes us feel good, even if that direction is probably not the direction the boss desires.

> Many bosses are unaware of the impact they are having on their team

For example, we will be motivated to look for another job or to take some other action which makes us feel better. When we are constrained from such action, because of the perceived limitations on our physical freedoms (for example, a lack of opportunities to change jobs) then we tend to draw upon our innermost emotional and spiritual energies to stimulate a sense of well-being. We dream, we fantasize and we draw immense succour from our friends and colleagues who are on our side. When our freedoms our limited the stimulus that motivates us in response to the atrocious behavior of a bad boss is not only the aspirational one (for example, the dream of winning the lottery) but the social one of interaction with friendly colleagues.

## Demotivation can exist alongside motivation

The paradox is that when people say "my boss demotivates me" they are actually being motivated to move in a direction away from their boss and his or her company. Thus a sense of demotivation can exist alongside motivation. The poor behavior of the boss can stimulates a sense of demotivation at the same time as stimulating the motivation to leave the company. It is only when there is no stimulus of freedom and we are totally restricted from moving away from feeling bad that a sense of permanent demotivation can set in.

The challenge, as stressed above, is to become aware at a corporate level as well as at an individual management level, of all those behaviors (policies, edicts, personal actions) which can stimulate bad feelings and therefore a dissipation of motivational energy into a thousand other directions. The challenge is also to generate as many corporate and leadership behaviors as possible that maximize the probability of stimulating a positive motivational response from employees.

Here are just five examples of such corporate and leadership behaviors that stimulate a positive motivational response:

▷ Sir Richard Branson of the Virgin Group throws open his home to employees every year (stimulus clusters: social, personal value).

▷ Kim Ward, Team Leader with WPA Medical Insurance, has introduced a game of "chance cards" to stimulate the motivation of her team. When the going gets tough each team member can draw a card which reveals one of a variety of rewards (e.g. "achieve target today and come in late tomorrow" or "have a lollipop") (stimulus cluster: diversionary).

- HSBC runs a program every 18 months called "the Winning Team" aimed at stimulating the motivation of all their employees (stimulus clusters: aspirational, diversionary, emotional, learning, social).

- Bob Dickinson, President of Carnival Cruises in Miami, spends a lot of time walking round his ships, making eye contact with crew, addressing them by their names and listening to what they have to say (stimulus clusters: personal value).

- Tanya Pillay-Nair, Front Office Manager at the Grand Hyatt Hotel in Singapore has created a scheme called "Magic Moments" to stimulate staff to create "magic" for their customers. When staff have create 16 magic moments for customers they receive an award (stimulus clusters: altruistic (do best for customers), personal value and inspirational).

## A stimulus–motivation biopsy

An exercise you might consider undertaking is a "biopsy" of your own corporate or leadership behavior, in order to identify the various subconscious and conscious stimuli that affect the motivation of your people. The purpose would then be to eliminate the negative stimuli and focus on the generation of positive stimuli.

Follow these steps:

- Write down a sample of your own corporate or leadership behavior (e.g. the way you greet people in the morning with just a cursory wave).

- Discover (or predict) the response of your team to this behavioral stimulus (e.g. they just give you a perfunctory nod).

- Judge whether this stimulus is positive or negative (e.g. probably negative).

- If negative, eliminate this behavior from your repertoire (e.g. stop this form of greeting).

- If positive, consider the possibility of replacing it with a fresh stimulus (e.g. try to greet people by name and stop by to ask them about themselves).

- Repeat this process for as many samples of your behaviors as possible (e.g. the way you communicate formal matters, whether or not your door is left open, how you react to people interrupting you, who you have lunch with etc.).

It is impossible to carry out a biopsy on all your behaviors at work. However, by selecting a small random sample you should reveal some fascinating information about the way you stimulate people. In doing so you will be able to identify those "poisonous" or "pathogenic" negative stimuli (such as ignoring people, or frowning at them) which risk damaging your relationship with them. Furthermore, the biopsy will help you identify those stimuli which are more likely to evoke a positive response. If you are really brave you could involve your team with the biopsy.

> Every decision, action, behavior and utterance by a manager contains a negative or positive stimulus potential

It should be stressed that every decision, action, behavior and utterance by a manager contains a negative or positive stimulus potential. Thus a new policy from head office will always contain a stimulus potential, not just in the substance of the policy but also in the way it was developed and subsequently communicated. The same applies to all decisions made by senior managers or at the front line by supervisors, together with all aspects of their informal behavior and communications.

Thus when a boss returns from an important meeting what he or she does immediately afterwards has the potential to stimulate the motivation or demotivation of the people around. Which options do you choose in such a circumstance? Ask yourself:

▷ Do I wander around giving some informal feedback to the team about the meeting?

▷ Do I convene a formal team meeting?

▷ Do I ignore my team and pick up the phone to make a call?

▷ Do I check the e-mails?

▷ Do I go through the in-tray?

▷ Do I go straight to my next meeting?

▷ Do I chat to my secretary?

▷ Do I call someone into the office to report on progress on another issue?

Each option is a potential stimulus to motivation or demotivation. These behavioral choices are typical and every day every manager will be faced with many such choices, each of which will act as motivational (or demotivational) stimuli. Even the absence of any such behavior, for example the absence of a boss, can act as a stimulus.

## All behaviors have the potential to stimulate a motivational reaction

Whatever your decision and subsequent behavior you choose, it will have the potential to stimulate a motivational or demotivational reaction from your people. Unless you are aware of this potential, the risk is you stimulate a negative reaction by default.

This potential is exaggerated when a new boss takes over. People watch his or her every move, looking for signals (stimuli) which might reveal the new person's approach. Ideally they are looking for a positive approach that will stimulate their own motivation. First impressions are no more than the result of the initial behavioral stimuli emitted by two or more people on first contact. They can arise from the look in a person's eyes, the warmth of greeting, the interest shown, the sound of a voice, the degree of expertise revealed, together with the level of confidence shown. The successful leaders are those who are aware of this and who allow their warm hearts and positive spirits to show through in the minutiae of their behavior and in their attempt to stimulate a positive reaction from their new teams.

> Bosses who are pre-occupied only with their own thing are rarely interested in the things that either motivate or demotivate their people

There are few leaders who excel at this stimulating approach. You might care to review your own personal experiences with the various bosses you have encountered in your life, whether you have reported to them directly or otherwise. How many have stimulated a positive response within you? In my own experience the number has been relatively small. Too many bosses I have met have been more interested in themselves and their own roles in the company than in me as a person. Too often I have sat down with senior executives who have been happy to wax lyrical about the issues that occupy their minds but who take little interest in anything else, let alone me. Whilst what they say can occasionally be stimulating, more frequently it evokes a negative response because they fail to take interest in the person to whom they're talking. Bosses who are pre-occupied with their own thing are rarely interested in the things that either motivate or demotivate other people. It is all of these things which act as stimuli and when the direction is one way (everything is directed to what is on the boss's mind) there tends to be a negative polarization.

# A paradigm shift: reversed motivation

A paradigm shift in motivation occurs when there is a reversal in the direction of stimulation. The previous pages of this chapter might have led you to the conclusion that the prime role of a leader is to stimulate the motivation of his or her people. Whilst it is a critical role, when it comes to motivation it is not the *only* role. The additional role belongs to the people and the way bosses allow themselves to be stimulated.

Great bosses will encourage their people to stimulate them with lively debate, great ideas and stories of successes. Great bosses allow their people to impress them rather than seek to impress their people. These bosses want to be influenced by their people, persuaded by them, convinced by them. They want to be advised by them as well as inspired by them. These bosses want to see the results of their people's creative enterprise and dedicated hard work. They want their people to surprise them and from time to time take their breath away. Great bosses want to join in the celebration of their people's achievements as well as support them in the resolution of their problems. The glory belongs to the people and this stimulates the bosses. These bosses love nothing better than to tell everyone of their people's accomplishments, of the way they defeated the odds, overcame adversity, conquered Goliath. Great leaders are overjoyed when someone comes to them with a positive story, of how they overcame a problem, of how they pleased a customer, of how they delivered the impossible, of how they exceeded all expectations. It is this manna from heaven that stimulates the best leaders.

> Bosses should allow people to stimulate them

These bosses are reluctant to take command and issue instructions, and perhaps only do so in times of crisis. They know that instructions, commands, edicts and the formal force of their own decisions are dangerous as stimuli and risk a negative reaction. Few people, once they know their jobs, like to be told what to do. The best bosses therefore encourage their people to take command and use the force of their own heartfelt decisions to achieve what they believe has to be achieved. These bosses know that four of the most powerful stimuli are drawn from the clusters of aspiration, emotion, freedom and personal value. If it's what the people want to achieve, from the bottom of their hearts and they have the freedom to make the appropriate choices, then they are more likely to achieve it than if they are restricted by the instructions of a dictatorial boss.

In other words, a company is more likely to achieve a result when it is what the employees want to achieve. The boss's role is secondary in providing emotional support through such stimuli as learning, discovery and reward. The bosses facilitate the learning process by which employees enhance their value with increased experience, knowledge and skills. The bosses stimulate their people's attention by questioning them and helping them discover solutions to their own problems. Furthermore, such bosses love nothing more than rewarding their people with a display of how they really value their endeavors and their accomplishments.

> Four of the most powerful stimuli are drawn from the clusters of aspiration, emotion, freedom and personal value

So leaders stimulate their people to stimulate them. It is a two-way process, perhaps initiated by the bosses but then taken over by the team who have the prime role to accomplish what they believe is necessary and then to stimulate the bosses by soliciting their support, encouragement and appreciation.

When the process of mutual stimulation begins to take place then the organization begins to buzz. It is "a.c." as opposed to "d.c." and so much more powerful as a result. The effect can be electric. Everyone is energized because everyone energizes each other with positive stimuli. The bosses radiate positive energy and this is transmitted through the teams, who stimulate in turn the radiation of new energies. When the bosses light up everyone lights up and this makes the bosses shine even more.

In those companies where morale is low the light is dimmed because the bosses do not shine. Energies are not sparked because the bosses themselves are not sparking them. When you shine a light on success you will see success. But if you have no light to shine you will not see anything. The leader's role is to shine the light, show the way and then see their people sparkle. There is no other way. It is their way. That is the key stimulus.

# 7

# A stimulus
# for change

We are fanatical about our core values. I've been with the company
12 years and not one day have I missed pulling out the core values
and asking myself, can I improve, can I change? I also challenge
my team. We spend a lot of time reflecting on these core values.
We go over them time and time again – and eventually they rub
off and there is a change. Behavior changes and attitude changes.
*Nick Clayton, General Manager, Ritz Carlton Hotel, Singapore*

## Straight lines are not natural

Here is a little exercise I have yet to set at one of my seminars. Go to the
nearest bathroom, strip off and examine your naked body closely to see if
you can identify a straight line on it. I defy you to find one. Everything about
your body will be crooked and curved. Nature does not produce straight
lines. To prove this, walk to the nearest park (it would be wise to get dressed
first) and carefully study the trees, the leaves, the birds, the flowers, the
blades of grass, and once again see if you can identify a straight line. I defy
you to find one. Nature does not produce straight lines. Everything that
grows naturally is curved or crooked.

In fact straight lines do not exist in this world – except as figments of our
imagination. Everything we think of as straight is in fact an artificial product
of mankind, for example a ruler, the edge of a book or a table, a line drawn
on a piece of paper. Even so, such straight lines are not really straight, they
are approximations to straightness. We just interpret them in our minds as

straight. If you draw what you think is a straight line and then examine the line under magnification you will find it very furry and far from straight.

We thus allow ourselves to be deceived when we think that many things in life are "straightforward." Managers are particularly prone to this deception. They think they can set a goal and then a set of actions that will lead straight to the goal (*see* Fig. 7.1).

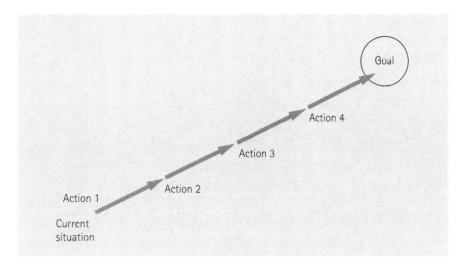

**Fig 7.1**

Setting a "straightforward" goal

## Drawing the line with scientific management

The problem with "scientific management" is that it attempts to establish straight lines between cause and effect by way of analyzes, formulae, rules, regulations and procedures. Managers are always trying to develop systems that comprise a series of straight lines that will lead a company from A to Z by way of B, C and D. Thus many management textbooks and training courses espouse a simple formula which comprises "the seven steps to success." Everyone is desperate for these simple steps because they want the ease of a straight line to follow.

> Linear thinking is of little use when dealing with people

Such linear thinking can be of use when dealing with inanimate objects such as computers and machinery. However, it is of little use when dealing with people and the organizations in which they work. Furthermore, it is of little use when attempting the management of change.

For a process of *impersonal* manufacture linear systems can be used to good effect: we can determine the shortest route for delivering a product from A to Z or we can determine the best way of producing item X for a customer in the shortest possible time. However, when it comes to relationships and the *personal* side of business then systemized linear thinking is rarely helpful. It is this personal side of change that is the subject of this chapter.

The delusion propagated in scientific management is that linear rational thinking, whilst applicable to the production and distribution of inanimate objects, is also applicable to relationships. This fallacy is at the root of most failures of organizations to adapt and change. This view is shared by Howard Sherman and Ron Schultz (1998) who state:

The difficulty is giving up the mechanical, logical progressions of the Industrial Age and having to enter a world of nonlinear thinking. For hundreds of years, business has assumed that the target it was trying to hit was something "out there." All a business had to do was aim at the target and progress along a straight and narrow path until reaching it.

When it comes to persuading customers to buy, suppliers to supply and employees to comply, then linear thinking (such as bureaucratic procedures for communication, goal setting and performance appraisal) should be thrown out of the window. Relationships between people, and particularly between employees and their managers, evolve in the same way that animals and plants evolve in nature – in a slow incremental non-linear fashion.

> Relationships between employees and their managers evolve in a non-linear fashion

Everything in nature grows by way of a complex series of minute responses to a vast number of external stimuli. Nature has no system but chaos, but out of the chaos patterns emerge, which we call trees, birds and everything we know as living. A large number of starlings will emerge from the trees into a pattern we call a "flock." The flock will not fly in a straight line but swirl around in the air. Who decides the direction? Do they have a leader who sends signals: "turn left," "up a bit," "down a bit," "straight on," "squawk now." The answer is no. As David Whyte (1994) has pointed out, the pattern of movement results from one small stimulus, a change of direction by one bird, leading to an immediate response by the adjacent birds. These immediate responses in turn become the stimuli for the birds adjacent to them. One bird starts veering to the left and that influences the next bird and so on. In a football crowd it is called the 'Mexican wave." Thirty thousand people will wave in a particularly timed sequence in response to a stimulus originated by a small group of people.

## Organizations change in a non-linear way

Organizations of people thus respond in a natural but complex way to stimuli. However, they do not respond in a linear way and managers would be unwise to believe that they can effect change by relying solely on a series of logical actions such as announcements, roadshows, workshops, goal setting, feedback loops, consultation programs and so on. There is a risk that the response will be the obverse of that intended: "Oh no! Not another initiative from head office!"

To quote from one of my earlier books (Freemantle, 1995):

Most managers and their people are fed up to their back teeth with the latest initiative from the center, telling them how to do their job. These initiatives are often from self-righteous, inexperienced, empire-building centralists who delude themselves into thinking that they know best. They attempt thought reform, attitudinal change or behavior improvement with the use of whizzy techniques. There are reminiscences of Chairman Mao as the edict is issued: "You must think *quality*" (as if we have never thought *quality* before, as if we have never done anything about quality in our lives, as if the thought of implementing total quality was an amazing gem of wisdom from our esteemed chairman who is fighting a heroic battle against the enemies of the organization who seek to destroy it with substandard production). ... "You must think like the Chairman, *quality* is important."

Forty years before that was written, William Whyte (1956) wrote: "The organization man is one who has left home, spiritually as well as physically, to take the vows of organization life and it is they who are the mind and soul of our great self-perpetuating institutions."

William Whyte was only partly right in 1956 as I was only partly right in 1995. As soon as you have someone who has been changed into an "organization man" then there is no way you can continue as a self-perpetuating institution. The largest airline flying across the Atlantic in 1982 was PanAm. Where is PanAm today? Where are the retailers of my childhood, the Hepworths, the Dolcis and the Fine Fares? Where are the Berni Inns and the Ritz Cinemas? No organization is self-perpetuating and the danger is that if you try to change your people into "organization people" by persuading them or forcing them to adopt a set of organization vows then you risk the very future of your business. When a company tries to change its people they will find it very difficult to change the company.

During this first year of this millennium three incredibly reputable organizations suffered relatively poor results. The first is that flag-waver for British retailing Marks & Spencer. The second is an airline that was excep-tionally successfully in the 1980s and set itself a reputation for being the world's favorite airline: British Airways. The third is BMW, who acquired Rover, struggled with it for a few years and then struggled with a very public disposal of the UK car manufacturer. It wasn't so long ago that IBM, an icon of best management practice in the 1970s, was struggling for survival. In this last case IBM had a clearly defined approach to management which it expressed as the IBM way. This embraced such admirable principles as respect for the individual, service to the customer, excellence as a way of life and effective leadership. Yet in the late 1980s and early 1990s IBM experienced a range of major problems.

> When a company tries to change its people they will find it very difficult to change the company

Observing these major organizations fighting for survival in an increas-ingly competitive world I kept on asking myself "Why didn't they change? Why didn't they adapt?" In nature those animals and those plants that survive are those that adapt to the environment by responding effectively and as necessary to the changing stimuli in the environment. The question is not a new one. Writing in the 1980s Rosabeth Moss Kanter (1984) said: "Recent business history is filled with the skeletons of companies that failed to innovate or even to recognize the need to adapt to obvious change."

Most organizations at some time or another have been through "major change programs" assisted by experts from outside. So why did Marks & Spencer, British Airways, BMW and a few years earlier IBM fail to adapt and change in order to protect their profits and more importantly the jobs of their people? Surely these major companies could afford the very best expertise available in the world? Surely they could have hired in the top business school professors to advise them? Perhaps they did. But as James O'Shea and Charles Madigan (1997) point out you can spend half-a-billion dollars on consultants and achieve nothing as a result.

# The failure to adapt and change

The problem of failing to adapt and implement change in organizations is due to one overriding issue. It stems from applying an impersonal approach to what is a personal issue for everyone involved. It is relatively easy to change equipment, to bring in the latest technology and apply the latest computerized techniques, but that is not the "change" to which we are referring in this chapter. Most people nowadays accept such changes and are willing to work with new technology. The much greater challenge, and the one referred to here, is how to change people when a new approach and culture is required to meet the demands of the marketplace. To change people involves changing their thinking, their attitudes, their feelings, their emotions and therefore themselves. The challenge of organizational change and therefore "changing people" is incredibly complex and not as simple as following a logical set of linear procedures, the likes of which you come across in many textbooks on change. That is why most "change programs" fail. An article by Michael Beer and Nitin Nohria (2000) states:

> Failing to implement change in organizations is due to applying an impersonal approach to what is a personal issue for everyone involved

Despite some individual successes change remains difficult to pull off and few companies manage the process well. Most initiatives – installing new technology, downsizing, restructuring, or trying to change corporate culture – have had low success rates. The brutal fact is that about 70 per cent of all change initiatives fail.

This is of course despite the fact that innumerable books have been written on the subject and very few so-called "professional managers" have learnt the clear lessons from them, including the one put forward in the early 1980s by Rosabeth Moss Kanter (1984):

A tradition of success via the efforts of individuals is found in American corporate history. Many companies have "forgotten" this, stifling much individual initiative … The task of stimulating more innovation is a difficult one … barriers of communication, structure and reward exist.

One of the best case studies of successful change is that of British Aerospace. To quote the Chairman Sir Richard Evans (1999), using a couple of metaphors from nature and science:

Real change can only grow out of the soil on which each individual stands … Leaders influence culture through the neurons of the organization. They do not bark orders: they create connections and relationships that spur efficiency, innovation and other intended behaviors and attitudes.

## Partial stimulation

Therefore to initiate and accomplish change you cannot rely on a few written declarations of intent backed up by a few training workshops. This is "partial stimulation." To effect change you must have "total stimulation" by which every single thing senior executives and managers do and say reflects the intended change. The change must radiate out from the very people insti-

> Before you can change an organization – and before you can change other people – you have to change yourself.

gating the change, rather than be seen as a part-time exercise left to others to administer. The leaders of the change process must live and breathe the change by changing themselves. Too many bosses continue with their old traditional habits whilst declaring that they want employees to acquire and practice "new thinking." For example, too many bosses declare that they want their employees to be "empowered" at the same as they, the bosses, continue with the old approach that disempowers employees. These bosses "intellectualize" the change and come up with reasons for it, but fail to emotionalize it. They try to stimulate the change intellectually without even trying to stimulate it emotionally. The reason is that they fail to take the change into their hearts and souls and therefore fail to change themselves. Before you can change an organization – and before you can change other people – you have to change yourself.

Recently I was with a client in the transport industry. It was explained to me that they were embarking on a "change program" for inspectors. Previously the role of their inspectors had been seen as one of revenue protection. Inspectors would inspect tickets and and get their brownie points for discovering passengers who did not have tickets or who had paid the wrong amount. In other words inspectors had a policing or controlling role to protect the company from all these crooks trying to exploit it. Now the senior management wanted to change the role from revenue protection into one of customer care. The prime role of the inspectors would no longer be to chase money but to assist customers. Each inspector would be attending a two-day training workshop to help them understand the new role. That was it. The logic relating to the new role and how to implement it was irrefutable and was a product of linear thinking (go from role A to role C by way of training workshop B).

The trouble was that senior management were having little to do with this change and still behaved in a way that was consistent with revenue protection and inconsistent with customer care. By showing little interest in the program and by still behaving in a way that was counter to the logic of the program senior managers were sending out signals or stimuli that evoked a different response to that intended. They evoked a response of confusion, negativity and distrust. Inspectors still feared they would be pulled up if they did not discover passengers trying to ride with paying. In other words whilst they were expected to change, they did not seeing anything changing in the management's approach.

A more positive example is given in the book *The Soul at Work* (Lewin and Regine, 1999):

John's presence was pivotal to stimulating a cultural change. It was John's way of being with them that instigated the change. There were four behaviors that he demonstrated: being open, straight, human and in relationship. These behaviors proved to be very effective in convincing a skeptical culture that things could and would be different.

Another company, a hotel group, approached the need for change in a different way. It convened a group of people to explore the options for change, given the dynamic marketplace they were in. Outside experts were brought in to stimulate some thinking about the various possibilities for pushing back the boundaries. The unpredictable outcome of this initial session was that the group effected some changes immediately, whilst other changes were recommended to senior executives. The immediate changes and the recommendations acted as stimuli for further debate and further action out of which a number of changes were made which were not originally thought of at the first session. The changes that evolved were both minor and major, ranging from the way guests were greeted and the way toilets were cleaned, to some major changes to the group's product portfolio.

> The key is that change is evolutionary and has to be sparked

## The law of unintended consequences

The key is that change is evolutionary and has to be sparked. The consequences of such evolution and such sparking are rarely known – it is what I have described as the law of unintended consequences. Most people would prefer the benefit of intended consequences ("We go for a vacation and the intended consequence is that we will be relaxed, happy, eat some good food and see some interesting sights") whilst in reality many of the consequences are unintended ("We met this most fascinating person on vacation").

The consequences of organizational change are rarely predictable. Whilst it is quite logical to create an intended consequence in terms of a vision or a goal, frequently an unintended consequence results ("I was surprised by the attitude of the people in ...").

The initial spark for change normally comes from an external stimulus. For example, the inspiration for the chain of Starbucks coffee shops came when Howard Schultz, now Chairman, was in Milan in 1983:

Whilst in Milan I noticed a little espresso bar. I ducked inside to look around ... it was great theater (the way the *barista* served coffee). As I watched I had a revelation. What we had to do was unlock the romance and mystery of coffee, firsthand, in coffee bars. (Schultz, 1997)

That initial revelation sparked a revolution in the way coffee is sold and drunk in this world. Starbucks are everywhere, even here in Windsor where I live in the UK. They are in Beijing, Singapore and many other places. Many other companies have also tried to emulate them.

## The spark that initiates change

An initial spark can light a fire in someone's belly. In turn, this fire can ignite excitement and enthusiasm throughout an organization, energizing people to make changes. Richard Dawkins (1996) gives a good analogy:

Imagine a dry, parched grassland, stretching for mile after mile in every direction. A lighted match is dropped and in no time the grass has flared up into a racing fire. The fire doesn't just swell steadily outwards from the original starting point. It also sends sparks up into the air. These sparks are carried by the wind. When a spark eventually comes down it starts a new fire. The new fire then sends off sparks which kindle yet more new fires somewhere else.

Organizations are often dry, parched grasslands stretching for miles. They can be destroyed by fire or they can put the energies released by the fire to positive effect – for the benefit of their customers as well as employees and shareholders. The key is to create the sparks and stimuli that can energize people into making such changes. Our modern business heroes, such as Sir Richard Branson, Herb Kelleher, Jack Welch and a few others, are those who create sparks to energize people. When people are energized change comes

> When people are energized change comes naturally as they use the energy to adapt to the environment

naturally as they use the energy to adapt to the environment. When they are not energized they effectively become parched or (to mix my metaphors) frozen. People become locked into the rigidities of rules, regulations, routine and convention. They thus become unable to adapt.

## The butterfly effect

Analogies from nature are all around. James Gleick (1988) popularized the term "butterfly effect" to describe the way a butterfly flapping its wings could affect the weather thousands of miles away: "In science as in life it is well known that a chain of events can have a start point of crisis that could magnify small changes." In organizational terms the CEO has only to shout at a colleague for the effect to be felt throughout the company. Certain stimuli will energize a ripple effect throughout the company, causing it to move in a certain direction, intended or otherwise.

For example, the recent decline in the fortunes of British Airways could be attributed to the ripple effect of a number of such stimuli emanating from the previous Chief Executive. The repainting of tailfins on the company's aeroplanes caused a ripple effect and led to an unintended consequence of adverse reaction, as did decisions to reduce commissions for travel agents and impose new working practices for employees. In each of these examples the stimulus was not just the decision (which possessed immense linear logic), but also the way the decision was communicated and implemented. To quote journalist Nigel Coombs (2000): "The Chief Executive lacked the personal touch that made it possible for his predecessors to push through unpopular decisions." A "personal touch" is a stimulus that is of immense importance when initiating change. A strategic decision for change implemented with an impersonal touch is much less likely to be successful than the same decision implemented with a personal touch.

## The amoeba effect

Another natural analogy for viewing an organization is that of the amoeba. An amoeba moves in various directions in response to specific stimuli, sometimes joining up with other amoebae, sometimes splitting from them. The history of Rover cars is an example (*see* Fig. 7.2).

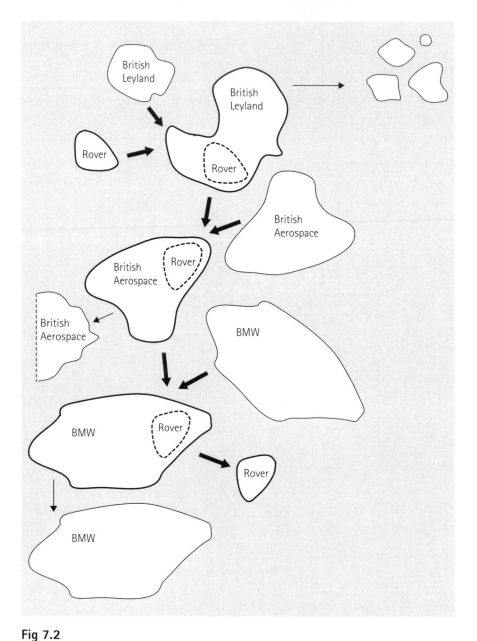

**Fig 7.2**

The amoeba effect

The amoeba effect can be seen in many companies in terms of partnerships and alliances with others, as well as in splits from them. It can also be seen within companies in terms of the constant re-organization that often takes place. One minute human resources is a stand-alone function, the next minute it comes under finance and administration. The amoebic organization keeps moving, sometimes merging with others, sometimes splitting, sometimes remaining alone.

"The momentum to effect change can snowball out of quite modest beginnings" wrote Sir Michael Edwardes (1984), who was in charge of British Leyland back in the late 1970s and early 1980s and who was reputed to be one of the best company managers around the time. Yet not even he (nor I suspect British Aerospace and BMW subsequently) was able to foresee the direction Rover cars would take. The direction eventually taken – a series of unintended consequences – was in response to a number of stimuli. Some of these were impersonal, such as exchange rates, and some were personal, such as the responses of customers to the model range, the desires of the people owning and running these companies, as well as pressures from the employees themselves, not to mention the influence of politicians.

## Change through total stimulation

It is therefore difficult to predict the outcome of change, even if there is a vision of desired change. To maximize the probability that a vision of change is realized, a senior executive can only rely on creating as wide a range of positive stimuli as possible to ensure total stimulation of the amoeba-like organization. Partial stimulation, whereby the process of change is sidelined from mainstream activities, is doomed to the fate of being one of the 70 per cent of change programs that fail.

This chapter is about how organizations and their people might change, not how equipment, plant, machinery and buildings change. The total stimulation required to change organizations and their people means that everyone, from chief executive officer to switchboard operator, will need to reflect the required changes. Change is a dynamic, interactive, two-way process involving everyone. If reason does enter into the process, and it should if we are take full advantage of all our faculties, then the prime motive for change must be external. Animals adapt to their external environment, modifying their feeding habits and behaviors as necessary. Similarly, organizations need to adapt to their environment by beating off the competition for scarce resources (revenue from customers). Starbucks adjusted to the environment by turning coffee making into a great performance or theater. In doing so Howard Schultz (1997) stimulated the motivation of an ever increasing number of employees:

The brand is much more than a cup of coffee – it's the experience. The most important component in our brand is the employee. They are at the top of the triangle. The people have created the magic. The people have created the experience.

## Using magic as a stimulus for change

Magic is a stimulus. A boss can create magic for employees and employees can create magic for customers. To quote Jean Carvalho, Executive Vice-President with BankAtlantic in the USA, speaking of her President, Alan Levan: "Alan makes me feel that there's nothing I touch that I can't turn to magic. Therefore I have no option but to turn it to magic. I have to make magic for him."

By selecting a range of positive stimuli a senior executive can conjure up an organization that is magic in the eyes of its customers and employees. Magic at first seems irrational. People cannot believe their eyes. Magic has hidden secrets revealed to but a few exponents of the profession.

But magic is not so magic. It is an illusion. Everyone can practise magic. Our lives at times are so humdrum, so full of repetitive routines and mindless habits that when someone does something special for us it seems to be "magic." By definition, change cannot be effected by a continuation of repetitive routines and mindless habits. For change to work, therefore, it has to be something special in the environment that triggers the process of adaptation, which in turns creates something special by way of adaptation.

# The origin of the need to change

The real need for change does not originate from the chief executive or the boss. They merely perceive it, articulate it and then stimulate the process by which it takes place. The real need arises from the ever changing world around us – the internet, e-commerce, global telecommunications, new competition,

External changes necessitate internal changes

the evolution of new consumer habits (for example, drinking cappuccino and caffe latte). It is the world that is external to us that sparks the change and forces us to adapt or die.

The changes that need to take place do not just relate to new products, new services and new markets but in the way we think and feel about the business we are in and its customers and employees. External changes in the environment thus necessitate internal changes within us as individuals and within our organizations. Furthermore, when things go wrong internally and there is a need to change, we often externalize the problem. To quote Robert Quinn (1996):

We cannot easily recognize that the problem is part of the system in which we play an active role. Our first inclination is always from a perspective that externalizes the problem, keeps it somewhere "out there." Because the problem is "out there," it is always others who need to change ... In our attempts to address such problem situations, we usually begin by telling these persons what the problem is and how they might change.

## External and internal change

The relationship between external change and internal change is thus critical. External stimuli will trigger internal changes and conversely internal stimuli will trigger external changes. Each one of us is part of the change process. Too frequently I hear people arriving late for meetings and blaming the traffic: "Sorry I'm late, the traffic was dreadful this morning." What they are not prepared to accept is that there are certain people, like me, who are never late for meetings, irrespective of traffic conditions. When people blame the traffic, they are externalizing *their* problem.

> Most people can solve more problems than they think they can

We like to blame others. We like to accuse the politicians, or the highways engineers, or the large trucks, or the school buses for clogging up the roads. The change to our traffic problems will actually come from within us – not just from politicians. I walk to the station. I use trains whenever I can. I work at home. My 30-year-old daughter Kate even cycles across London for 40 minutes to get to work. We can all solve our traffic problems by applying our minds and feet. Most people can solve more problems than they think they can – if only they would change to thinking that way!

Thus to effect change we must change ourselves, using a combination of both external and internal stimuli. The external stimuli to change us can arise from the environment, our colleagues or our bosses. Similarly, we can behave in a way that stimulates change in others. We can it make it fun for people to work in our department, we can develop a "feel" for what is going on, we can listen and understand whenever necessary, we can take an interest and try to make people feel special. We can change from being shy and reserved to being happy and outgoing, we can change from being indifferent and disinterested to being enthusiastic and willing. We can change from being passive to proactive, from being quiet to communicative, from being cold to warm. We can spend more time with people and change the way we schedule our day. We can change our priorities from paperwork to people, from counting beans to being accountable to customers. We can become more curious and ask more questions, we can strive to learn even more. We can work smarter and set ourselves impossible challenges ("Who said it's impossible to put a man on the Moon?").

We must change ourselves if we are ever to survive in a fiercely competitive world. We cannot wait for others to make the changes for us; in fact, they are making the changes for themselves.

## Change means changing our own minds, hearts, souls and behaviors

To change ourselves means not just changing our behaviors but changing our minds, our hearts, our spirits and our souls. Too often I hear people tell me of how they want others to change. It is always someone else who should do this. It is never us. We know best. The stimulus is to challenge that "best" – to discover an even better way.

I don't know best. In a previous book (Freemantle, 1995) I wrote: "The drums are banged, the 'think quality' posters are put up, and hordes of red guards are mobilized through expensive thought-reform programs of education." The implication was that you should not bang the drums, should not put posters up and that you should not have expensive thought-reform programs of education. I was both wrong and right. Of course you should have all these things to stimulate the organization to change, but it would be wrong if that was all. Just to have these things would be "partial stimulation." Ideally these whizzy activities should be part of the "total stimulation" that takes place.

**If you are unhappy with people's behavior you have to change their thinking. To change their thinking you have to change the way they feel. To change the way they feel you need to change the people themselves in terms of the spirit that resides inside their hearts.**

To achieve any change in another person, therefore, you have to stimulate a change of heart. Have you experienced a change of heart over recent times? Have you experienced a change in the way you feel about certain people, certain customers, certain companies and certainly yourself? If you have not been stimulated to have a change of heart, how do you think others can do so? In other words, our own personal changes become the essential stimuli for other people's changes. When a new boss replaces an old boss people find the change quite stimulating. The change itself stimulates change. If you are an existing boss you will not be able to change your team unless you change yourself.

## The stimulus of behavior and emotion in making changes

In practice this means that if you want to change from an autocratic process-driven organization into a customer-oriented company with a progressive approach to people management, then first of all you have demonstrate in a genuine way that you are customer oriented and a progressive people manager yourself. You will only change people when your own behavior reflects the changes you espouse. In this sense your words will have a mere secondary role. Words alone are far from sufficient in stimulating change. Much more stimulating are the behaviors and emotions you use to support the words you utter, as well as the deeds you undertake. When you put emotion and spirit into your words and actions, you will be much more stimulating than if you just act in automatic mode.

This means you must examine every facet of your daily management behavior and communications, with a view to factoring into it a positive emotional stimulus that will energize others. As soon as people are convinced that you have changed then you will be able to stimulate a genuine debate throughout the organization of what this means in practice to everyone else. The end result of such a debate might be the adoption of new practices and the pursuit of improvements which had never occurred to you in the first place. To quote John Harvey-Jones (1988): "It has to be possible to dream and speak the unthinkable, for the only thing that we do know is that we shall not know what tomorrow's world will be like. It will have changed more than even the most outrageous thinking is likely to encompass."

A boss is not the sole custodian of the unthinkable and the outrageous; in fact, far better if such thoughts emanate from the team than from a senior person. In this way a boss can be stimulated by the team. The boss stimulates the debate and the team stimulates the boss with ideas which push back the boundaries. Everyone then puts the ideas into practice and that is the change required.

The pitfall is when the obverse happens – when there is a reliance on linear thinking by which senior executives envisage the change required and then try to explain it to everyone by means of roadshows, workshops, fancy posters or whatever. Too many employees in too many organizations are sick to death of the exhortations and propaganda to which they are subjected in vain attempts to brainwash them into the new way of thinking, in order to facilitate change.

Change in large organizations therefore evolves incrementally in response to a number of stimuli, all drawn from the 17 clusters of motivational stimuli. It evolves from the stimulus of debate in response to stimuli from the external environment. It evolves from the stimulus of curiosity and the resultant learning. It evolves in response to the stimulus of the magical models displayed by our heroes and heroines. It evolves in response to our emotions, for example the fears generated by external threats and the fears that we are being left behind or that the competion is taking over. It evolves when we step outside our shells and are forced to respond to an invigorating and stimulating climate. It evolves when one small behavioral stimulus (for example, an apocryphal story about the CEO) leads to another small stimulus, which in turn leads to a series of stimuli that energize the people in an organization. It evolves from the incidence of opportunity or the creation of it, for example when we encounter something unexpected, or see things differently, or when an idea just bubbles up.

## Change is natural, change is constant

Change is as a natural as the movement of an amoeba, or the flapping of a butterfly's wings, or the swirl of a flock of starlings, or the burning of prairie grass, or the evolving contours of our landscapes and townscapes. Nothing stays still for long. Have a look at your own body. Have a look at your local park. Have a look at your organization. You will find it under constant change and you will find it stimulating. If you reflect long enough you will discover that actually you have stimulated more of the change than you thought. By creating an awareness of the way change is stimulated you are in a position to stimulate change yourself.

> By creating an awareness of the way change is stimulated you are in a position to stimulate change yourself

This does not mean to say that all change happens by default as a result of natural evolution. Change can be initiated with positive outcomes and this can apply to ourselves as individuals as well as to organizational change. The two are closely related. The following sections examines how the process of "stimulus transfer" effects organizational change.

## Stimulus transfer and change

Successful organization change is dependent on stimulating a number of "positive carriers" who can retransmit the stimulus to other people.

For example, a new chief executive might wish to "change" an organization towards direction Y (where for example Y might be "front-line empowerment") as opposed to the current X situation (where decisions are made centrally at high level). In fact Y could represent any change initiative, whether it relate to improved customer service, better quality, greater creativity, more teamwork or partnership working.

The first time the chief executive communicates the message (for example, "We need Y-type 'front-line empowerment'"), each recipient of the message will respond to the stimulus according to the binary code of motivation. The response will either be:

- "Y makes me feel bad (I will therefore resist it).
  Negative response: "I will block Y and stay with X although I might 'pretend' to go along with Y" (blockage or partial stimulation).

- "Y makes me feel good (I will therefore go along with it)."
  Positive response: "I will accept Y and behave accordingly, retransmitting Y to others as appropriate" (total stimulation).

This can be demonstrated in an individual case as in Fig. 7.3.

With an increasing number of recipients it is virtually impossible to predict who will respond positively to the Y message and who will react (X) negatively. What people say is no indication at all. Too many people are subservient and acquiescent and will merely intellectualize the message without changing their behavior. In other words they will attempt to regurgitate the message on the assumption that this will be sufficient to change others' behavior. However, regurgitation of the message is a very weak stimulus and is effectively "lip service." The most powerful stimulus for transfer is an individual's behavior as a reflection of their own heart and soul. The message has to be supported by genuine emotion and spirit. Y people practise what they preach rather than just preach.

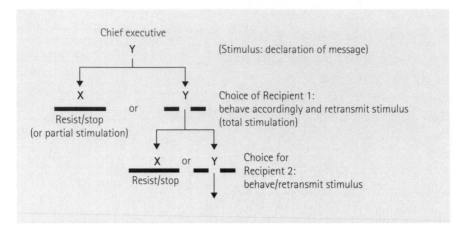

**Fig 7.3**

Responding to a stimulus

At the start of any organizational change process there will be relatively few positive carriers of the stimulus. Even so, the stimulus will transfer to certain people who will then respond. By repeated stimulation, an increasing number of people will change from X to Y and fewer and fewer will resist.

This is indicated in Fig. 7.4 where each X represents an individual who resists the message stimulus and each Y an individual who accepts it and retransmits it. Each line represents a situation where an individual responds positively to the stimulus (flowing down the organization hierarchy). Where an arrow is shown, the stimulus is upwards or sideways in the hierarchy.

When the attempt to change takes place through total stimulation there is a greater probability that more people will respond with a Y and that they in turn will then become positive carriers for the stimulus. The direction of the stimulus transfer rarely follows hierarchical lines and can be upwards (an employee stimulates a manager to change), horizontal (peer group transfer), diagonal (from one department across to another), as well as downwards (a manager inspires a team to change).

Experts on how large numbers of people change their behaviors in a similar direction would assert that the transfer (from X to Y) throughout a population is random, although facilitated by a number of carriers. One such expert, Malcolm Gladwell (2000), would call these people "connectors." These are people with a very powerful Y influence and therefore transmit

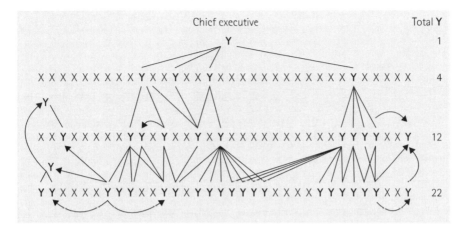

**Fig 7.4**

Responding to a stimulus in an organization hierarchy

strong stimuli which influence many within their sphere. It is difficult to find out and identify who these powerful positive carriers of the stimulus are. They do not always declare themselves and the way they transmit the stimulus is not always verbal but often behavioral. As a result, other people respond by emulating their Y-type behavior.

The issue of change is one where simple linear logic is rarely effective and where a whole range of stimuli (drawn from the 17 stimulus clusters) might combine to create a powerful stimulus to effect. The stimulus must also be varied from time to time. This does not mean to say that the message should change, but that the way the message is transmitted should change. Logic is a relatively weak stimulus and can only be amplified by the power of emotion and spirit.

> Logic is a relatively weak stimulus and can only be amplified by the power of emotion and spirit

As more people switch from X to Y a critical mass will suddenly develop at an undefined moment of time – this is frequently between six to nine months after the initiation of the change program. The critical mass is created when suddenly a large number of people who have repeatedly resisted the Y stimulus (and variants of it) suddenly switch to it. They might have blocked the Y stimulus on 99 different occasions but on the hundredth occasion they "suddenly see the light of day" or "see how the land lies" and switch to Y. The critical mass effect is demonstrated in Fig. 7.5.

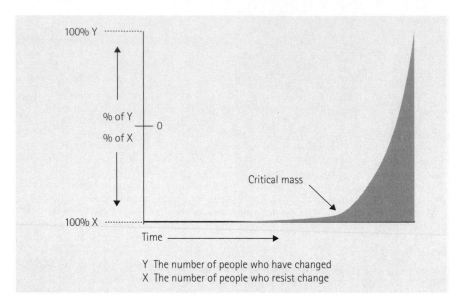

**Fig 7.5**

Stimulus transfer – the critical mass affect

The critical process of stimulus transfer in effecting organizational change is akin to the amoeba effect and the butterfly effect. In the first case one small stimulus can cause the large amoeba to move in a different direction, in the second case one small stimulus can create a much larger outcome far away.

## A blueprint for organizational change

Having railed against the application of linear thinking to the process of changing organizations and people I am reluctant to offer a pat set of steps to expedite such change. However, Table 7.1 offers some considerations as a blueprint for the process of change you wish to stimulate.

## Table 7.1

### A blueprint for organizational change – some considerations

| Consideration | Example of response (and related stimulus cluster) |
| --- | --- |
| What is the change you require? | We need to be more customer oriented (*aspirational*). |
| | We have lost sight of our core value of putting the customer first and need to reinforce this (*aspirational*). |
| What external stimulus is sparking this change? | We need to be ahead of competition and this will help us make a difference (*aspirational*). |
| Is there an internal stimulus too? | I fundamentally believe this is the right thing to do. We need to do more for our customers (*spiritual*). |
| What stimuli should I use to initiate the change? | I need to examine and challenge my own behaviors, thinkings, feelings, beliefs to identify the changes I should make personally (*learning, discovery*). |
| Give an example | I need to make more time for customers (*social, altruistic*). |
| | I need to be more creative in making them feel special (*inspirational*). |
| | I need to treat my team the same way (*social, altruistic*). |
| | I need to ensure all my behaviors and communications reflect the importance of customer orientation (*spiritual*). |
| How will you stimulate the debate about change? | I will arrange a series of half day sessions at which I will pose the question (how do we become more customer oriented?) and listen to the responses (*discovery, learning*). |
| | I will encourage people to take the appropriate action (*freedom*). |
| | I will also pursue the debate informally by creating opportunities to meet as many people as possible (*social*). |
| What additional stimuli will you use? (how will you vary the stimuli?) | This could well be subject to the outcome from the previous communication sessions. However I intend to encourage the celebration of success when changes are made, I will support people in their requests for more training, better equipment (*reward, altruistic*). |
| Any other stimulus variants? | I will bring in some outside experts to expose my team to the latest thinking (*discovery, learning*). |
| | I will encourage my team to visit other companies which are models of success (*diversionary, discovery, learning*). |
| | I will encourage them to spend more time with customers, as I will be doing and learning from their experiences (*learning*). |
| | Finally I will encourage the team to create an environment by which the approach is reinforced. I will suggest they design posters, balloons, have games, quizzes and so on to stimulate a continued awareness of the importance of this change (*environmental, achievement*). |

# 8

# The stimulus
# of new language

A vital stimulus for motivation, change and improvement is language. Unless we change the language we will not make the change.

## The importance of language as a stimulus

Drawn from the social cluster of motivational stimuli, language is an essential stimulus to achievement. Many of the motivational stimuli that can be drawn from the 17 clusters could not exist without the facility of language. Without language, our aspirations remain as pictures in our mind and cannot be shared with others.

> If we choose the wrong words, or say them in the wrong way, we are effectively choosing the wrong stimulus

Without the words "We'll put a man on the moon by the end of the decade." a man would not have been put on the moon. So if we choose the wrong words, or say them in the wrong way, we are effectively choosing the wrong stimulus and will not achieve what we want. We would not have the internet today unless someone had not coined the word "internet" in the first place. Before we had computers we had to have the word "computer." Without the stimulus of language we would still be apes with nothing but body language and a few grunts and squeals to go on. Language differentiates us from all other species and it is language that differentiates us from the competition, not just product and price. When we say "putting people first" we are using language to differentiate us from those businesses which "put money first." The change of one word can thus stimulate a process of major changes in the way business is conducted and people are motivated. It is the effective use of language in reflecting our personal values and aspirations that creates the necessary changes and improvements.

At an individual level, we often perceive a person who goes about their job at the front line without saying anything as indifferent and lacking in personality. Conversely, a person "with personality" is one who is able to express themselves in a positive way that touches the spirit of those people they are working with or the customers they are serving. When we peel away the emotions and the thinking, we will find that it is the effective use of language that reveals our souls – or attempts to cover them up. Without language we would not be people – the word "people" would not exist. It is language that makes us people.

## Language and communication

Whilst "communication" has been at the center of the management stage for half a century, the issue of language has been relatively neglected. I used to be a cynic on this issue. The importance of communication cannot be denied, but underpinning it is the use of language and it was this use that frequently made me angry. I would rail against the so-called gurus who grew famous by inventing new terms for the language of business management. "All they are doing," I would say to myself, "is using new labels whilst putting old wine into new bottles." What I saw these experts doing was focusing on some aspects of management which were obvious and commonsense and giving them newfangled new names and passing them off as the latest wonder-techniques. Who needed "MBO" (management by objectives), I asked myself, when the commonsense thing for any boss to do was determine what had to be achieved in the future? Who needed "performance appraisal" when it was obvious that employees should have feedback about how well they were doing? Who needed a "balanced scorecard" when it should be clear to any executive with at least one ounce of nous that there were three fundamental aspects of business that should be assessed? Who needed a "customer service excellence improvement program" when even an 11-year-old kid working on a school project could tell you that business was all about satisfying customers and exceeding their expectations? And, by the way, what do we mean by (i) satisfaction, (ii) expectations, (ii) appraisal, (iv) performance, and (v) objectives?

The consultants were having a field day inventing all this new language and then persuading clients to part with billions of dollars in a vain attempt to interpret and understand what this new concocted language or jargon meant. Someone would insert a new word like "empowerment" into the management vocabulary and then divert vast amounts of precious management and staff time to discuss what "empowerment" really meant in practice.

When it came to management speak, business jargon, buzz-words, acronyms, flavours-of-the-month or the latest fashions in management, I was a fully fledged cynic. Any reader of my previous books would have detected my personal rage at all this high-falutin nonsense. I prided myself on being a realist, on being a down-to-earth, no-nonsense person who spoke the language of the "man on the street" and had no time for these managers who lived on a different planet and spoke a language no one understood. My cynicism knew no bounds and I made a living out of it for a long while, lecturing audiences around the world on the need to get back to common-sense and to say "thank you" for a good job done, rather than rely on the bureaucracies of an inane performance reward system.

So behind their backs I debunked the experts and became an expert in doing so. Many shared my view and many still do. For example, a recent article entitled "Thought followership" in *The Economist* (20 May 2000) railed against consultants who call themselves "thought leaders":

Every few years or so, consultants and gurus look for a new phrase to describe what they have always been trying to do, namely helping people to run their companies better. Previous examples included "corporate re-engineering" and "searching for excellence." Hence also another recent habit, that of labelling a commonsense process with a baffling phrase, and adding a trademark to it.

Two years ago I would have agreed with this article, believing that all these people were inventing was a new language – they were developing techniques around the new words and phrases and then deluding themselves that they were making progress when all they had done was concoct jargon.

Having graduated in 1984 from the "University of Management Heretics" with a first-class degree in "Cynicism" I felt compelled to rid the world of business of all this brainwashing – to flush away the superficialities of management jargon and to help hard-pressed executives get back to the real world where their employees could understand what they were saying. In reality people did not have managers, or leaders – but they had "bosses."

This is how they spoke and this was the real world. So, falling into my own trap, I called my first book and then my company "Superboss."

Despite my valiant efforts the new management words and the new business techniques came along thick and fast and seemed to be increasingly popular. It was very difficult to market "commonsense" as I had been trying to do. I rationalized by telling myself that what these other gurus were doing was forsaking their principles, eroding their integrity and converting bite-size chunks (or "modules" to use some jargon) of commonsense into "packaged products" and selling these as the latest wondertechniques. Because I believed in commonsense and integrity I could hardly package this up into a nice little seller that came with six cassettes and a large box.

Such was my mindset. Cynicism was in my blood. People were losing touch with reality by playing with words. The "medium had become the message." To quote Marshall McLuhan (1994): "In a culture likes ours, long accustomed to splitting and dividing all things as a means of control, it is sometimes a bit of a shock to reminded that, in operational and practical fact, the medium is the message." McLuhan then went on to describe how the use of a medium extends people. In other words you cannot separate the message from the medium; the medium is part of the message. McLuhan gives the example of electricity as a medium. The mere use of this medium has radically changed the world – it has created a new message, even though in this case the medium, electricity, has no information content.

## The medium changes the message

McLuhan's book was originally published in 1964 and created a storm. When I revisited it in researching for this book it created a storm in my mind. Perhaps I had been wrong to rail at all those experts for inventing "management speak." "Management speak" is the medium and as a result the message has changed.

> "Management speak" has played a vital role in stimulating progress in business over the last 40 years

As a result of this storm I began to delve into some rather ancient management books (ancient in management terms) dating back to the 1960s – and I became increasingly convinced that I had been wrong. I became increasingly convinced that "management speak," rather than being superficial and alienating, has played a vital role in stimulating progress in business over the last 40 years.

For example, when I came across the following words they almost gave me apoplexy. I just could not believe what I was reading. These were words from Peter Drucker, the world's most famous management guru, an expert revered throughout the world as being a leading management thinker. Yet he wrote the paragraph below in 1967 in a best selling book on how to be a successful executive:

Time spent working with people is a central task in the work of the executive. People are time-consumers. And most people are time-wasters … Relations with knowledge workers are especially time-consuming. Whatever the reason – whether it is the absence of the barrier of class and authority between superior and subordinate in knowledge work, or whether he simply takes himself more seriously – the knowledge worker makes much greater time demands than the manual worker on his superior as well as on his associates. Moreover, because knowledge work cannot be measured the way manual work can, one cannot tell a knowledge worker in a few simple words whether he is doing the right job and how well he is doing it.

I'll repeat the negative stimuli that sparked my anger:

- "People are time-consumers"
- "Most people are time-wasters"
- "The superior and his subordinate"
- "A manual worker and his superior"
- "Tell whether he is doing the right job"
- "A few simple words (for the manual worker)"

After you calm down you might to care to reflect on the language used in 1967 by the world's leading management guru at that time. I can guarantee that it is not a language that any manager dare use today nor would want to. A further study of this 1967 book on management reveals little reference to "motivation" but excessive coverage of how to deal with time-wasters and feather-bedding. Here are two further quotes from this book:

- The effective decision-maker, therefore, organizes disagreement."
- "Effective executives know, of course, that there are fools around and that there are mischief-makers."

There is no reference in this book to vision, mission, emotion, quality, fun, a bias for action, customer service, values, positive thinking and a range of words that have now entered our management vocabulary and stimulated our thinking about motivation, performance and business progress.

This book is typical of the thinking of the time, as reflected in the language used. Another book of the time (Tillett, Kempner and Wills, 1970) on leading management thinkers concentrates on efficiency, the measurement of work, welfare and co-operation with trade unions. Again there is no use of the management words to which we are now accustomed. People did not talk about customer service in the late 1960s and early 1970s, nor did they talk of total quality management or motivation programs.

An even earlier book (Brown, 1960) on "new management thinking" has the following key items in its index:

- the executive system
- the manager and his subordinates
- policy making and its effects
- written policy and communications
- the representative system
- the legislative system
- the appeals procedure.

In the management thinking at that time everything was seen in terms of a system, procedure or policy. There are plenty of references to: "sanctions," "appeals," "command," "authority," "meetings," "role definitions" and "standing orders." Management in the 1960s was seen as a matter of efficient administration, dealing with people through unionized procedures. There were few, if any, references to customers or customer service. In fact the term "customer service" did not exist then. The language and thinking of management evolved from the Industrial Revolution and the challenging task of how to administer factories with increasing numbers of "workers."

In the first half of the nineteenth century thinking about factory administration was stimulated by the writings of Max Weber, Frederick Winslow Taylor, Henri Fayol and George Elton Mayo. Terms such as "work study" and "welfare" entered the mainstream vocabulary for managers as they tried to apply the principles of "scientific management" to the "process" of "administering" industrial production. An issue such as "motivation" was dealt with in terms of the "welfare system," whilst the psychological aspects of people management were expressed in terms such as "procedures for testing attitudes, personality and intelligence" or "appraisal systems." There had to be a system for everything and an effective manager was one who effectively managed these systems.

It was not until Douglas McGregor came along in the 1960s that the use of this systems language for managing people was challenged. A further debate on motivation was stimulated by his theories on the X and Y styles of leadership. McGregor was one of the first management writers to introduce the term "emotion" into the management vocabulary. He stated that:

Some of my academic colleagues are fond of saying that emotion is a dirty word in management's lexicon. Management appears to want to eliminate the effects of emotion on behavior in the organization setting. The essential difficulty is that the typical managerial view of emotion is highly restricted. Human loyalty, enthusiasm, drive, commitment, acceptance of responsibility and self-confidence are all emotional variables. So are all the values "we hold dear." (McGregor, 1966)

In other words, according to McGregor emotion was an important force in motivation.

McGregor was ahead of his time and it was not until the late 1990s that the debate on emotion was further stimulated when Daniel Goleman (1996) introduced the term "emotional intelligence" into the management vocabulary. The abhorrence of emotion was still prevalent in the late 1980s, as evidenced in one of the first books using the term "customer service": "Now and then, especially if the customer is of the opposite sex, positive emotional response may endanger effective customer contact. We must maintain professional detachment at all costs" (Peel, 1987).

## The stimulus of new management terms

The boundaries of management thinking and practice are thus pushed back by introducing into the language the stimulus of new management terms. Hertzberg did it with his "hygiene theory," whilst Maslow did it with his theory on the "hierarchy of needs." In the 1980s Peters and Waterman did it by introducing managers to the term "excellence" whilst Senge did it with the term "the learning organization." By coining new terms to describe new thinking patterns, these gurus effectively created "short-cuts" which speeded up progress in the way managers applied themselves to developing their businesses. Without the use of the term "excellence" we would not search for excellence and thus we would risk not being excellent. Similarly, without use of the term "the learning organization" we would probably not challenge our own organizations on how we learn and thus we would risk not learning. Equally, if it was not for the "balanced scorecard" we would probably focus all our attention on measuring revenue, costs and profit and neglect to measure the key factors relating to people, customers and innovation. Back in the 1970s John Humble stimulated new management thinking with his approach to "management by objectives" (MBO), as did Bill Reddin did with his "3-D" approach to management styles.

Whilst new management terms always risk being rejected as "jargon," many of them prove more durable and actually stimulate a debate which broadens the boundaries of effective management practice. Here are some terms (in random order) which you will not find in the management text books 30 years ago but which are now widely used:

- fun
- Wow!
- excellence
- core values
- culture
- mission
- the balanced scorecard
- continuous improvement
- promise
- customization
- creative thinking
- target setting
- customer intimacy
- self-managing teams
- comfort zones
- SWOT
- 360° appraisal
- the inverted triangle
- customer service
- customer care

- focus groups
- mystery shopping
- emotions
- exceeding expectations
- putting people first
- facilitation
- best practice
- bias for action
- performance indicators
- principles
- buzz
- passion
- vision
- beliefs
- change management
- the learning organization
- chaos
- commitment
- mindset
- performance measurement
- customer interface
- close to the customer
- self-esteem
- pushing back the boundaries
- critical success factors
- climate surveys
- empowerment
- total quality management
- customer relations management
- customer satisfaction

- competencies
- emotional intelligence
- going the extra mile
- management by walking around (MBWA)
- workshops
- value for money
- needs analysis
- stakeholders
- philosophy.

This list, whilst appearing awesome, is far from comprehensive. The benefit of using such language is that it forces the debate "What does this mean in practice?" For example, only by using the term "empowerment" can we attempt to define what it means in practice and therefore put it into practice. Whilst it is quite possible to have an empowered organization which does not use the term, it will not be conscious of its empowerment unless it uses the term. Alternatively, it might use other terms such "trust" or "ownership" or "delegation," which are variations on the theme.

An example of the use of language to stimulate a debate about best practice comes from the Ritz Carlton Hotel Group, which calls their employees "ladies and gentlemen." The Group has a "credo" which states that the genuine care and comfort of our "guests" is our highest "mission." It also has an "employee promise" and a set of "basics," which form the basis of its exceptionally high standards. Thus it is the language of "core values" that stimulates practices which both employees and customers value. The Ritz Carlton Group has daily "line-ups" at which the practical application of the "core values" is reviewed with all "ladies and gentlemen." Thus Nick Clayton, General Manager at the Ritz Carlton Hotel, Singapore, uses the opportunities of these "line-ups" to inspire staff to accomplish the hotel's "vision" and apply the "core values."

## The way language is used – the emotional conduit

The language is the stimulus that sparks the motivational drive to improve performance. However, it is not the words alone that create the stimulus but also the way they are used. Left alone with its words (vocabulary) and structure (grammar), language is merely a string of two-dimensional expressions in the form of phrases, sentences and paragraphs. To be effective in eliciting a response, the language stimulus has to be amplified by the third dimension of emotion. Too often statements of "mission" and "core values" are merely hung on walls, where they gather dust but little else. Words alone achieve nothing unless they are channeled along an emotional conduit that connects with another person. The use of the words therefore has to stimulate that emotional conduit and this can only be achieved by adding the appropriate emotion to the words.

> Words alone achieve nothing unless they are channeled along an emotional conduit that connects with another person

For example, the UK chain of Prêt à Manger states on its packaging that it has a "passion for food." These are just words unless there is a genuine passion, felt by managers and employees alike, for food. From my experience as a customer of Prêt à Manger, that passion genuinely exists not only for food but also for customers and for people. To quote from the company's "philosophy": "We are passionate about food, our staff and our customers. If there is a secret to our success so far, it's probably our determination to put quality before profit. Quality, not just of our food, but in every aspect of what we do." The statement is succinct and clear enough for everyone – for customers to understand and for staff to apply. By articulating a "philosophy" of "quality before profit" the company can stimulate a debate amongst all as to what this means in practice. These practices are then spelt out in a number of "Prêt Passion Facts" such as "Prêt avoids the obscure chemicals and preservatives commonly used to extend the shelf-life of food." The company then goes on to state: "Our sandwiches are freshly made one by one in each shop … We don't like sell-by dates. At the end of each day we offer all our unsold sandwiches to Crisis Fareshare to help feed the homeless." Thus the "philosophy" of "quality before profit" extends in every aspect of its "practice." The language used stimulates the practice. When there is no language available to express "philosophy" and how it relates to "practice" then the probability is that everyday practice will *not* relate to philosophy.

The use of language therefore enables us to create a conscious awareness of existing philosophies and practices and to stimulate a debate on how to improve. Whilst many practices exist "naturally" without us having a conscious awareness of them, we can only develop the practices by creating such awareness. Language facilitates this process.

## Converting abstract concepts into practice

To create this conscious awareness we need to resort to words that are effectively abstract concepts. If I say to you "apple" you will immediately form a picture in your mind of an apple. The picture becomes clearer if I say "large red apple". With concept words such as "trust" and "empowerment" it becomes much more difficult to create pictures which we can convert into practice. When I make the request "Please buy some large red apples at the market," the pictures created in your mind will be clear and explicit. However, if I say "I wish to empower my team," the picture is less clear and thus stimulates a thought process to determine what "empowering my team" really means in practice.

Most relationships between people are dependent on practices that can be clustered under the banner of a concept word. Thus the word "communication" indicates a concept within which are a variety of behaviors, such as speaking, telling, hearing, listening, conveying a message, writing and consulting. The same applies to many words in the "language of relationships." To enhance our relationships we need to resort to these concept words. There is nothing new in this. Socrates, as indicated in the early Dialogues, spent much of his time questioning people as to the meaning of such words as "goodness," "bravery" and "courage." To improve our relationships at work and in business we will thus need to resort to abstract concept words in order to explore the practical meanings of such improvements. Socrates relentlessly grilled people like Laches and Charmides to discover what they meant, in practice, by all these fine words.

We need to find out, too, although the words have changed. We no longer demand "bravery" in the workplace, although "goodness" and "courage" still have application. But we do need to question what abstract words like "performance" mean in practice. Unless we do so, there is no way we can improve performance. Unless we use the term "appraisal", there is no way we can identify practical ways of appraising performance. To push back the boundaries in developing our businesses we thus need to resort to new concepts and therefore new words and phrases to establish the practice. That is why the Ritz Carlton Hotel group uses the phrase "ladies and gentlemen" to refer to its employees, whilst the ASDA chain of stores uses the term "colleagues." Other companies like John Lewis and Starbucks use the term "partners." In replacing the more traditional words of "employees" or "staff" a debate is stimulated in the workplace. After all, it was only 30 years ago that we referred to employees as "workers."

Think about the implications of using one of the following terms:

- human resources
- personnel
- employee relations
- welfare
- industrial relations
- staff
- colleagues
- associates
- partners
- people.

What are the practical differences between these ten terms? Many would argue that the term used by any one organization reflects the values of that organization. Thus many executives I interviewed abhorred the term "human resources." To quote just one, Jonathan McMillan of Schering-Plough:

There was a time when I was hideously demotivated to the point of depression. I had a good manager. I was part of a big company that ceased to consider us as people. We were the "human resources" (to be listed along with coal, gas, oil – to be exploited until something cheaper came along). I was number 46115 to that company. I still remember the number. Previously if I rang up Personnel they would know my name. Then they changed "Personnel" to "Human Resources." When I rang up "Human Resources" they wanted to know my number. I was a number to them. I looked for another job.

In other words, by using new concepts we have to define what they mean and the process of defining can be accomplished by describing the actual practice. The medium becomes the message. The meaning evolves out of the practice as a result of the new language which has stimulated it.

## The stimulus of new language in making strategic and operational improvements

The stimulus of new language in facilitating progress applies at a strategic level as well as operationally on a daily, behavioral basis. A company might well create a strategic "leadership through quality" campaign which stimulates the evolution of practices which lead to high quality. The phrase "leadership through quality" creates a three-word stimulus which enables people to focus on the strategies necessary to maintain and improve quality.

> Not only do we have to choose words that stimulate people but the emotions that support those words

On a daily basis, the "leadership through quality" stimulus enables people to focus on their own attitudes and behaviors in delivering high quality. Again, it should be stressed that as words alone the statement "leadership through quality" is meaningless unless it is amplified by the display of genuine emotion from the heart, together with a positive spirit reflecting the values of the organization and its leaders.

## The stimulus of emotional undertones and overtones

Ultimately all communications act as stimuli competing to elicit a desired response. By delicately loading our language with feelings and spirit we can open up an emotional conduit which connects with others and maximizes the chance of the desired response being obtained. Not only do we have to choose words and phrases that stimulate others but we also have to choose the emotions that support each word and phrase. This choice extends to every single word we utter. Thus there are a wide variety of choices in the way we say "Yes", as indicated in the ten examples in Table 8.1.

**Table 8.1**

**Ten different ways of saying "yes"**

| Emotion | Short-cut | Extended version |
|---------|-----------|------------------|
| Reluctance | "Yes!" | "Yes, I agree if you insist!" |
| Acquiescence | "Yes" | "Yes, I agree because it's you, but it's not what I want" |
| Irritation | "Yes?" | "Yes, what is it?" ("Interrupt me if you insist!") |
| Desire | "Yes!" | "Yes! This is what I want!" |
| Excitement | "Yes!" | "Yes! We've scored!" |
| Delight | "Yes!" | "Yes! Of course you can!" |
| Uncertainty | "Yes ..." | "Yes ... but I'm not sure" |
| No emotion | "Yes" | Unthinking, unfeeling automatic response to simple question |
| Enthusiasm | "Yes!" | "Yes! Let's do it!" |
| Satisfaction | "Yes" | "Yes. I'm pleased this has happened" |
| Emotion + word = stimulus (conveying feeling + logic) | | |

Therefore it is not just *what* a company says to its employees that is important but *how* it says it. "How" it says it reflects the emotions (or lack of emotions) of its leaders and it is this "how" stimulus that is vital in eliciting the desired response.

Given the number of words in the English language and the various ways of combining them, together with the wide range of emotional undertones and overtones we can use, there are an infinite number ways of expressing ourselves in any given situation. Steven Pinker (1999) has estimated that the English language has the potential of 6.4 trillion different five-word sentences. He goes on to say: "Suppose it takes five seconds to produce one of these sentences. To crank them all out would take a million years." However, it is common for sentences to have 20 words or more. Pinker therefore estimates that "there are about one hundred million trillion of them [possible 20-word sentences] in the English language. For comparison, that is about a hundred times the number of seconds since the birth of the universe." Pinker does not take into account the emotions that can be employed to vary the meaning of any one word. There are therefore an infinite number of languages options we can choose to express ourselves and stimulate a response from another person. So why rely on repetition and bore people stiff?

And meanwhile the boundaries of language are being pushed back by the continual introduction of new words and phrases! We have already seen how the idiom extant in the 1960s has dramatically changed to an extended vocabulary of terms now used by the modern manager. You might think it not possible for the vocabulary to change further, but I forecast that you will see the following words play a major role in stimulating the debate about progressive management in the coming decade:

- challenge
- aspiration
- soul
- spirit
- stimulus
- energy
- integrity
- outcome
- people
- freedom

- ▶ "being oneself"
- ▶ happiness
- ▶ imagination
- ▶ heartware
- ▶ fantasy
- ▶ added emotional value
- ▶ imagination
- ▶ choice
- ▶ support
- ▶ uniqueness (as an individual)
- ▶ discovery
- ▶ family
- ▶ flexibility
- ▶ inner rewards
- ▶ self-motivation
- ▶ questioning
- ▶ adventure
- ▶ colleague
- ▶ warmth
- ▶ Yes!

The most effective leaders are aware of the stimulus of language and how the words they use in everyday communication (whether speaking or writing or by e-mail) must be reinforced with energies from their hearts and souls, as well as focused on the vision and values of the company. For example, the words "putting people first," when heartfelt and reflecting a boss's individual values, will stimulate behaviors at nine o'clock on a Monday morning that demonstrate that the boss puts people first. Speaking at the Institute of Directors Conference in1999 Tim Waterstone, founder of the Waterstone's chain of bookstores in the UK, stated: "Every morning I try to write six postcards to members of staff. If I pass a Waterstone's window that has a particularly good display I write to them. I try to say thank you all the time."

In other words if you believe it you say so, and if you say so you do it.

# Challenging the words you use

When you are trying to improve performance, or to make a change, or to stimulate the motivation of an individual or team of people it is worth challenging yourself on the words you use in everyday language. The danger is that you are using the same old words to say the same old things and are thus failing totally to stimulate the desired response. To elicit the desired response and create something new you should experiment with the use of new language. Try to reflect the concepts you have in mind for the future, together with your genuinely held values, with a new expression that has the potentially to connect emotionally with others.

Thus one of my clients, an Asian company, has introduced the concept of "YES!" ("Yes! to Exceptional Service") to stimulate a debate on how best to ensure that its service provision stayed at number one position in customer ratings. The objective was to deliver service "from the heart." The "YES!" logo included an emblem of the heart. Another client, a British company, is pioneering an approach entitled "Beyond Service" to encourage thousands of employees to push back the boundaries in serving their customers. One chief executive with whom I am working is using the term "heartware" to stimulate a debate on how to add emotional value to the way the company deals with customers. These are but three examples of how new language can be used to stimulate the motivation of employees to make improvements.

> To create something new you should experiment with the use of new language

The use of these new high-level terms acts as an effective "short-cut" and focus for progressive change. The debate is stimulated, which in turn stimulates understanding of what these concepts mean in practice. The practice follows from the stimulus of the new language. The practice leads to learning what the original terms means. Nobody can know for sure what the "YES!" program, or "Beyond Service" or "heartware" actually means until they actual put it into practice. The proof of the pudding is in the eating. The meaning of the new management language is in the practice.

## Refreshing the language you use

In addition to introducing new language to reflect a company's strategic thinking for the future, individual managers should aim to do the same to reflect their own thinking when communicating with their teams. This context does not necessarily mean using new words and phrases that do not exist in the extant management vocabulary but words and phrases from the existing idiom that an individual manager rarely uses. These might be such "new" words (new to this specific boss) as "please," "thank you," "Hello, how are you?" "I really appreciated that," "That was fantastic!"

The opportunities for leaping away from the habits and monotony of routine language use are infinite. Try using different words from those you normally use. Try greeting people in different ways or try to create a new expression for praising people or try using a different enquiry when showing an interest in them. When the language you use becomes repetitive and predictable it loses its ability to stimulate people. A repeated "thank you" becomes meaningless. To stimulate that warm glow inside a person you need to create a new way of saying "thank you" every time.

Before practising this at work you can try practising it at home. Try speaking to your partner using subtle alterations in words and phrase. He or she will think you are a new person and will love you even more as a result!

> We need to keep our relationships alive and fresh by stimulating them with new expressions – which reflect our new thinking

When was the last time you told your partner that he or she is "one in a million"? If you have not used this term recently use it today – providing it genuinely reflects your feelings. If you use the term regularly, try a different stimulus; for example, tell your loved one "you are a star!"

Now try to identify a new language stimulus for giving positive feedback to your team at work. Tell someone: "You're a genius for cracking this problem!" or "That was magic!" However, do not use the terms "genius" or "magic" too often. The stimulus effect wears off quickly. You will constantly need to be seeking fresh language to keep the relationships with your team fresh.

So, we have to "refresh" the way we speak and work. We need to get out of the old habits of always speaking the same old way and saying the same old thing. We need to keep our relationships alive and fresh by stimulating them with new expressions – which effectively reflect our new thinking. By developing our use of language we actually develop our own thinking and feelings. Furthermore, we develop our understandings of the world and its people. When our language ossifies it reflects the deterioration of our thinking and the closing up of our hearts. Conversely when we freshen up our language we will find that we are effectively revitalizing ourselves with new thinking and livelier and more positive hearts.

# Simple rules for using language as a stimulus

There are a number of simple rules in the world of business about using language as a stimulus. The first set of rules relates to "corporate language" and the second set relates to "individual language." Corporate language is what is used formally in every aspect of a company's "strategic" communications, whether they be with customers, suppliers, shareholders or employees, whilst individual language is what is used informally in the everyday communications between managers and employees.

## Corporate rules for using the stimulus of new language

- Reflect new strategies with new words.
- Use as few words as possible and keep the new message simple (e.g. "YES!").
- Ensure your corporate values are clearly articulated using language that is unique to your company.
- Ensure all corporate utterances can be clearly related to these values.
- Remember that 100 per cent of the task of senior executives is communication and therefore involves the use of language.
- Keep developing your corporate language with the introduction of new words and phrases which more ably reflect your values and the way forward.

## Individual rules

- Reflect your values with the language used: ensure the words you use reflect not only the company's values but your own personal values. Should there be any divergence, open up a debate and continue it until there is convergence (as reflected possibly in new language).
- Avoid repetition: don't repeat the same old words time and time again. For everyday communications trying using new words and phrases to keep the relationship fresh. (The young Chinese woman who services my present hotel room has just told me that in Fujian they don't say "How are you?" but "Have you had breakfast?" or "Have you eaten lunch?" etc. Try something similar, for example: "Tell me, did you have a cooked breakfast this morning?" It might well get a laugh! However, do not experiment with the greeting given me by a senior Chinese executive yesterday: "Hello, nice to see you, what does your wife say about your stomach?")

▷ Put positive emotion into what you say: become conscious of your emotions and the way they act as undertones or overtones to the words you use. In doing so flush away the negative emotions and try to have all your words strengthened by positive emotions. In other words put positive feeling into what you say.

▷ Experiment with new language: try out new words and phrases when trying to stimulate the motivation of another. For example, instead of saying "I'd like to discuss and agree your goals with you" try experimenting with "I'm very interested in your aspirations and how you see the challenges facing you." Try eliminating words such as "No!", which act as a negative stimulus, and replace them with more positive words such as "I'll do my best for you."

▷ Listen and allow others to stimulate you: remember that one of the best ways of stimulating the motivation of another is to listen and to allow that person to stimulate you. Therefore seek new words and phrases that spark conversation and encourage a person to open up to you. For example, instead of saying "I would like some feedback from you about…?", try "I am keen to learn your opinion about…?" or "From the bottom of your heart how do you feel about…?"

## The importance of inconsequential communication

Ultimately we must question the whole purpose of language. In doing so we will quickly come to the conclusion that the use of much language appears to be inconsequential. Language is helpful in storing information and conveying instructions; however much of our conversation is concerned with conveying what appears to be useless information to other people.

A great deal of what is said to us we are not interested in and cannot remember after five minutes. You only have to listen to a couple of people chatting away to realize that often what they are saying is pointless, valueless and will have no influence or effect on the other person. Most of us spend a lot of time hearing other people speak but not genuinely listening to them. As a result, 99.9 per cent of the words we hear are forgotten immediately. The same applies to reading. I can read a novel and within a day forget the story line and who the main characters were. I can attend a lecture and barely recall what was said within half-an-hour of it being said. Occasionally, one or two keys points remain lodged in my memory.

In other words, we appear to be wasting huge amounts of energy with our inconsequential use of language. Nobody is listening and nobody is remembering!

So what is the point of using all this language if the immediate consequence is so minimal? Why not just go quiet and conserve our energies for uttering those words which have some practical application, for example: "I'll be late into work tomorrow" or "Could you please order me a Caesar salad for lunch"? Why waste our energies telling people things we know they are going to forget immediately? Furthermore, why waste our energies listening to people telling us things we are not interested in?

The answer is that it is not a waste. Whilst there might be no "direct" or immediate consequence in a certain communication between two or more people, there is a significant "indirect" consequence. The reason is that in many social encounters silence stimulates uncertainty, suspicion and fear. People feel uncomfortable with others who do not speak. When a person is

> People feel uncomfortable with others who do not speak

silent we do not know what is going on in their mind. Therefore we tend to guess and invariably come to such conclusions as "They don't like me", or "They don't want to speak to me" or "They are not interested in me." Such silence can thus stimulate a reduction in our self-esteem.

## Silence induces fear

When people don't speak to us we lose confidence in ourselves – we begin to think we are unloved and not valued as individuals. Silence can then stimulate negative emotions within us that we find difficult to flush away. Conversely, conversation can stimulate positive emotions, even if the conversation is meaningless and inane. So the use of inconsequential language is vitally important in stimulating social relationships. This argument can also be extended to the written or electronically transmitted word. It can give us confidence that we live in a society that generally subscribes to the norms and values we hold dear. In the absence of the inconsequential written or electronically transmitted word we would be ignorant of the forces in society that might impact us. Such ignorance would induce fear. In the absence of an extensive amount of unimportant information we would be confined to our own direct experiences and the daily encounters we have with our families and the people in the "village of our life." Unimportant, easily forgotten language, by way of conversation or by way of books, newspaper and television, enables us to extend the boundaries of our perception of the world and thus gives us confidence.

## The importance of using inconsequential language in management

This is vitally important in the world of management where communication is much talked about but much less often practised effectively. Too many people in large organizations go about their work in total ignorance of what is going on and with little knowledge of their bosses and how they think and what they intend to do. Informal interaction at work is therefore vital to warm up an organization, remove fears and give people confidence. It is pointless relying on the occasional formal communication by way of newsletter or bulletin, or on the formal meetings in which managers report to employees.

## A manager's prime task is communication

Communication at work has to be total. A manager's prime task is communication. A manager does not sweep floors, prepare the product, serve customers or count the money. What a manager does is communicate. Much of that task of communication will appear pointless – because it will be using inconsequential language which is forgotten tomorrow. But to cut out apparently inconsequential language

> Communication at work has to be total

and confine communication at work to "the points that matter" will create a cold organization in which people are frozen with fear. The use of inconsequential language is therefore a vital stimulus at work. It does not matter what you say – just say something. "Did you have a cooked breakfast this morning?" It is an inconsequential question with an answer that is inconsequential in terms of direct practical application. However, such interactions are vital in stimulating social relationships and creating the trust and confidence on which all successful companies are based.

## Small talk

Another term for inconsequential language is "small talk." Many busy executives do not have time for "small talk." However, those that go the distance are those who are skilled at "small talk" with a large number of people. "Small talk" enables relationships to be built over a long period of time – and evidence shows that long-term success in business depends on relationships.

# 9

# The stimulus
# of imagination

*Dreams motivate me. I have these dreams about what I want to
do. I then say "I can do this." I then work myself towards these
goals. I don't plod along doing mundane things. I believe a lot in
creativity. The future lies in creativity.*
*David Leo, poet and Vice-President of a major Singapore company*

Drawn from the inspirational cluster of motivational stimuli, the stimulus of
imagination is as important as the social stimulus of language.

Progress is a result of imagination and the way the images we create in
our mind are put into practice through the medium of language. Imagination
is therefore a vital stimulus to all aspects of motivation and effective business
performance. However, without practical application our imagination is no
more than a series of daydreams.

## Routine, fantasies and imagination

At one level routines are the antithesis of imagination. As we get into repetitive mode our senses dull and we stop thinking. We do what we have always
done and we tend to do it in an unimaginative way. Whilst routine is critically important in the exercise of administration and mechanics (for
example, in getting a passenger jet off the ground and flying it) when applied
to interactions between people the relationships suffers.

At a second level routine can be a driving force for imaginative ideas. The
main product of routine is boredom, together with an illusion of comfort.

However, another product can be the fantasies that drift in and out of our consciousness as we allow our minds to be exercised in the absence of external stimuli. The low energy mode of routine cannot be too prolonged without us effectively going to sleep, so we have to stimulate our minds with thoughts and often those thoughts are fantasies. A person who is imaginative is able to select those fantasies that have practical potential and convert them into behaviors that create a new reality. Such is the fantasy of travel and the reason I am writing this on yet another long-haul flight. The fantasy of distant exotic lands (in this case the Far East) can eventually lead to the reality of the adventure of the flight and the visit. Often reality is far divorced from the fantasy that stimulated its creation. The excitement of a flight to our fantasy world turns into the monotony of sitting in the same aeroplane for 14 hours. The boredom produced can only be relieved by further stimuli and further fantasies. Whilst in-flight entertainment provides that relief for many, personally I resort to a laptop.

We are driven by our fantasies and dreams. The images provided by entertainment, whether in-flight films, music, books or other media, provide the external stimuli which create these fantasies as we seek to migrate from the harsh reality of the world we perceive we live in to another, better world.

> Fantasy drives imagination which in turn drives the creation of an even better world

Fantasy thus drives imagination, which in turn drives the creation of an even better world. Frequently we fail and the reality we create for ourselves is far divorced from the fantasy we had of it in the first place. Our fantasy of the paradise beach with white sands, palm trees, clear seas and blue skies is in reality a beach afflicted with mosquitos, polluted seas and hawkers who pester you every two minutes. Our fantasy of falling in love with the most wonderful person in the world becomes in reality a strained and stressful relationship with someone who has another side we never conceived of in our dreams (just study the lives and loves of celebrities for evidence of this). We dream of the perfect world and imagine how we can achieve it. We never quite get there but en route we often take small steps forward. Such is progress.

Along with language our fantasies provide the stimulus for all practical improvement. Often these fantasies arise from the inspiration we receive from other people. For example, Matt Groening, creator of "The Simpsons" has stated that his inspiration not only came from his father, who was a film producer and an avid collector of comics, but also from such great cartoonists as Ronald Searle and Charles Schultz.

# Inspiration and fantasy

My own inspiration comes from a variety of sources, frequently from outside my own area of expertise. Recently I attended a concert conducted by Leonard Slatkin in which Evelyn Glennie played a new percussion work – *UFO* by the American composer Michael Daugherty. Not only did I find *UFO* inspirational but I was also moved by the honesty of Michael Daugherty in the pre-concert talk when he revealed how he felt in composing the piece and trying to improve it with each performance. My inspiration was emotional – it filled me with energy to work even harder on improving this very book. I had the fantasy of being up on stage too and discussing with some interviewer how I had conceived, written and improved this book. I had had a similar inspiration when I attended an event in which the great Chilean novelist Isabel Allende was interviewed. Her genius had sprung out of adversity. It was inspirational.

## Impossible fantasies and achievable ones

Fantasies frequently race through my mind. Some of the fantasies are impossible to bring to reality, for example seeing England win the soccer world cup or to live through a year without war and crime. However, some fantasies are within the realms of future reality, even if they are incredibly challenging. For example, I continue to have fantasies of being a successful author and speaker, of living in an even larger house and of having all the time in the world to write and to be with my family. From these fantasies I draw images that I strive to convert to reality. Recently I saw one of my previous books on sale at Changi Airport and now I can imagine seeing this one on sale there too. It is a fantasy of seeing my books on sale everywhere, of coming across them displayed in shop windows, of undertaking promotional launches and making television appearances.

There is a whole range of other fantasies I have about my life and work and the images I select from them provide the stimulus for me to move forward. For example, I am now returning on a trip not having seen my family for two weeks. As I fantasize about my homecoming I have images of the welcome I will receive from my wife and my daughters Ruth-Elena and Linnet at Heathrow and images of handing out presents when we get home. The images of gift giving actually lead to the selecting of gifts, each purchase accompanied by an image of the delight of the recipient. These images stimulated my behaviors yesterday as I put my working papers aside in my hotel room and headed for the shops to search out the ideal gifts. The fantasy of a happy family stimulates the progress which enables us to take steps towards it.

Similarly, the fantasy of a happy work situation stimulates the progress towards working with a motivated team who perform exceptionally well. If our fantasy is high profitability we will select images that relate to it – for example, of delighted shareholders and of accolades from the financial press. The images might also be of a lean, mean organization in which costs have

> Imagination is pivotal to all our creative efforts

been cut to the minimum. Such images will stimulate the behaviors that maximize the potential of achieving such profit. Financial success is created out of fantasy – through the images we select of the money we will make for our company and for ourselves.

Imagination is thus pivotal to all our creative efforts and actually is the process of drawing out (frequently from our fantasies) images of past or potential realities. There is no accounting for our fantasies, which tend to originate from the depths of our psyche. However, imagination tends to be more a conscious process in which we bring intellectual and emotional forces into play (*see* Fig. 9.1).

The process of image selection is vitally important in all aspects of our life and work. When a person is unimaginative it is because there is no image selection or creation and thus no subsequent conversion into reality. The filter shown in Fig. 9.1 closes up and all the fantasies are suppressed and possibly eliminated. At worst, the bottling up of fantasies leads to such pressure that the bottle suddenly bursts open and results in the types of atrocious behaviors we frequently read about in newspapers.

## From fantasy to imagination to practical reality

Not all fantasies are negative however. We can consciously influence our psyche and subconscious energies by developing aspirational fantasies in which we can imagine some incredibly positive outcomes. For example, if we aspire to exceptional service and have a fantasy based around this we can imagine that every time we (or members of our team) encounter a customer he or she will be delighted with the outcome of that interaction. The process is cyclical. The fantasy leads to images which can lead to practical outcomes. These in turn lead to further images and further fantasies (*see* Fig. 9.2).

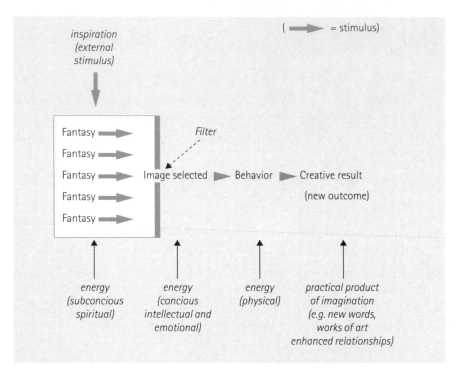

**Fig 9.1**

The process of imagination

## The difference between fantasy and imagination

It is important to stress the difference between fantasy and imagination. A fantasy is a whole set of freewheeling, uncontrolled images that occasionally surface in our minds as a result of internal or external stimuli. Some of these images are totally unrealistic, but there is the occasional one that can be selected as a basis for driving our behavior towards future reality. Imagination is the conscious process of selecting images (many originating from our fantasies) that drive our thinking and behavior. Thus we can have a fantasy of a happy family or a happy work situation and this could comprise a wide range of unrealistic and realistic images. We could fantasize, for example, that we would win ten million on the lottery and that we would make everyone in our family happy by buying them new homes, new cars and vacations to exotic locations. At work we could fantasize a situation in

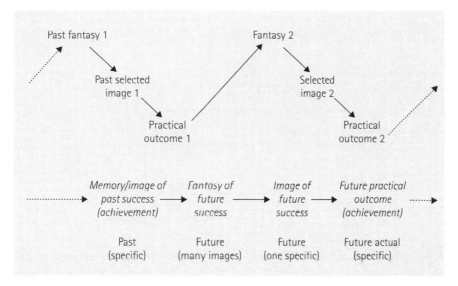

**Fig 9.2**

From fantasy to practical outcome

which the environment is perfect, the pay is phenomenally good, the customers are wonderful, our colleagues fantastic, where there are never any problems to stress us and where we always achieve what we seek to achieve. Such unrealistic images of paradise frequently float through our minds. However, they are occasionally interlaced with more realistic, if not challenging, images of the future, which we can select to convert into practical outcomes. The conscious rational processes in our mind carry out the task of selecting from the multitude of unrealistic images in our fantasies the one or two that we feel can be converted into a practical reality. Thus at one level we have a short-term fantasy of happy families and we select gifts for our loved ones, whilst at another level we have a longer term fantasy of career success and select the challenges we intend to meet to accomplish this.

An example from the business world is that of the California Milk Processor Board which, in 1993, was extremely worried about the free fall in milk consumption – a truly negative stimulus if there ever was one. The aspirational fantasy was to arrest the decline in milk sales through the stimulus of some incredibly creative marketing campaign. A number of agencies were invited to pitch for the work and amongst the many imaginative ideas put forward "GOT MILK?" emerged as the one that stimulated the best immediate response. The term, which emerged from an accidental slip of the tongue, prompted some of the most creative advertising in the history of American advertising and succeeded in arresting the decline in milk sales. To quote Jeff Manning (1999) who spearheaded the campaign: "GOT MILK? convinced me that creativity can't be taught. It can be encouraged and empowered, recognized and rewarded, but a person either floods the world with ideas or they don't." He goes on to say:

The GOT MILK? creative process taught me to cultivate risk. Risk is oxygen and adrenaline to the creative mind. It delivers a surge of energy. It sustains maximum effort in the face of exhaustion. It's the springboard for unprecedented performance. And it both whets and gnaws at the ego. People spend their entire lives being told not to take risks. Risk runs counter to stability. It increases the chance of mistakes. It can lead to damage and failure. It is, well, risky. What the world conveniently forgets is that normality is toxic to creativity, and risk is the fuel for anything exceptional.

The real risk is to tap into one's fantasies and select exciting images that will stimulate the world, push back the boundaries and attract more people. That's what GOT MILK? did.

## The influence on imagination of intellectual and emotional forces

The image selection process of imagination is driven by the intellectual and emotional forces of motivation – focusing us on "moving towards feeling good" and "moving away from feeling bad." It is these forces that we call our "motives" and to which we ascribe our reasons for everything we do. We select images that we feel stand a chance of making us and others feel good whilst rejecting images that might make us feel bad. If the practical outcome of our imaginative processes is that we and other people will feel good, then this will influence our subconscious fantasies. We will want more.

Imagination can be stimulated by any one of a wide range of stimuli drawn from the 17 clusters. For example, an aspirational stimulus can trigger a series of fantasies about golf, one of which might be to be another Tiger Woods whilst another, the one selected, might be to be the best golfer in one's local club. We can then create further images of how to achieve this, each image converted into practical behaviors that lead to the attainment of our aspiration. In terms of making improvements at work, a brilliant service experience we have had abroad can provide the inspirational stimulus that triggers a series of fantasies about our own customers enjoying similar experiences. From this we might select an image in which procedures are streamlined and the current hassle we give customers is eliminated.

In one recent case a team of maintenance engineers who serviced a company's fleet of industrial equipment (fork-lift trucks, hi-loaders, dollies, trucks, cranes, lifting gear, mini-buses etc.) was asked to fantasize about a future situation where the internal customers (the operations division) were perfectly happy about the service provided. Whilst the factory worked a three-shift system over 24 hours a day, seven days a week, the maintenance engineers only worked a two-shift system over 16 hours, five days a week, with the addition of emergency call-out. The exercise of fantasy yielded an image in which internal customers would never have to wait for days for an important piece of equipment to be repaired, as currently happened. The image of reduced delays on repairs led to the team of maintenance engineers proposing to its managers that it work the same three-shift system as its internal customers in operations. This was agreed and implemented.

## The two levels of imagination

The process of imagination operates at two levels: high level and low level. The latter relates to our everyday behaviors whilst the former relates to the grand strategies we formulate for our lives and work. For example, high-level imagination should apply to strategies, such as:

- stimulating the market
- progressive policies (e.g. personnel)
- working practices (e.g. rosters)
- training (imaginative programs)
- customer service (major initiatives)
- communication (formal)
- vision (long-term aspirations)
- environment (design, décor)
- approach (values, the way we do things, e.g. code of conduct)
- growth (company).

Low-level imagination should apply to daily behaviors, such as:

- stimulating our colleagues (greetings etc.)
- celebrating daily successes
- informal operational improvements
- learning (curosity etc.)
- customer service (minor initiatives)
- communication (informal)
- vision (short-term aspirations)
- environment (daily state)
- style (expressing the values, e.g. our actual conduct)
- growth (personal).

Virtually everything we do provides us with an opportunity to be imaginative – to do something in a new and better way. The way we great a colleague can either be imaginative or repetitive. The way we conduct a meeting can also be imaginative or repetitive and the same applies to writing reports, communication sessions, speaking on the telephone, sending e-mails and most of the things we do every day at work. When we bring our imagination to bear on what we do we are often reliant on the stimulus of language to facilitate communication (*see* Chapter 8). The stimulus of new language and the stimulus of imagination are closely interlinked.

> Virtually everything we do provides us with an opportunity to be imaginative

## The application of imagination at work

### Imaginative minutes

Recently I was in a meeting with a project committee that a client had set up to explore ways of improving service. I was shown a copy of the minutes of the previous meetings. These minutes were so boring as to be virtually useless. They were mere one-line statements of facts such as "Joe X reported that Department Y had been informed of initiative Z." I crave to see a set of imaginative minutes in which the essential record of a meeting is supplemented with some imaginative writing that assists effective communication and reflection. That will stimulate people!

## Imaginative formal presentations

I am tired of seeing the same old monotonous presentations using Power-Point formats with six bullet points to a slide and the same background for each slide. Where's the imagination, the color, the images, the interest?

## Imaginative meetings

I long to attend a regular management team session at which people are excited and some imagination comes into play in the way the meeting is conducted and the way ideas are communicated. Where's the music? Where's the opera? Where's the theater?

## Imaginative performance at work

Where's the imagination in the way we perform at work? When we put imagination into what we do we stimulate the emotional energies of others, we excite customers and employees alike and this in turn pushes back the boundaries of what is possible.

Ken Lockett plays the track "Proud" from the Heather Small album "Proud" to his team of branch managers. What did you do yesterday to make yourself feel proud? On previous occasions he played R. Kelly's "I believe I can fly."

## Imaginative strategies

At the high level, imagination must come into play in the way we develop our long-term strategies. If a company's strategic plan is boring then in all probability the outcomes it is striving for will be unimaginative. They will merely be logical extensions of the current situation or statistical projections. We need to liven up our strategies with emotional color so that all employees are attracted to them and energized to implement them. It takes imagination to develop a business, not just logic.

> If a company's strategic plan is boring then in all probability the outcomes it is striving for will be unimaginative

## Imaginative service

Here I am sitting in a business-class seat on a long-haul flight and thinking why does every airline I have ever flown with in business class merely offer a choice of three juices only: orange, apple or tomato? Why not occasionally offer something imaginative – like soursop, guava, lychee, mangosteen, apricot, grape, calamansi or even lime juice? These are juices that are readily available in the local stores of the country I have just visited. Also why not offer some interesting mineral waters, for example delicately flavoured with oldenlandia or chrysanthenum – both of which are inexpensive and again available in the local stores? You can argue as long as you like with explanations such as "Weight restrictions limit the range of juices we offer" but unless you experiment with imaginative new ideas you will never find out. Doesn't this airline have a fantasy about delighting me so much with its imaginative approach that I would never want to try out a competitor? It could at least experiment with one new juice and one new mineral water. At least Virgin experimented with in-flight massage and Sir Richard Branson walked the aisle performing magic for his customers.

## Imaginative guidelines

Companies cannot leave the process of imagination to chance, hoping that some bright employee might occasionally come up with a wonderful idea which is processed through the suggestion scheme for an eventual $200 award. It rarely happens. Companies wishing to push back the boundaries of customer experience by innovating with new products and services, strategically and operationally, need to create the environment in which both high-level and low-level imagination flourishes. Here are some guidelines for creating the conditions in which both high-level and low-level imagination can be stimulated.

### 1 Create a relaxating environment

Imagination can rarely flourish under the stress of a busy schedule. When an employee is under pressure to deliver operationally, or a manager is rushing around from one meeting to another, the image filter closes up – the individual's energies concentrate on the task in hand rather than an image of the future. Time therefore needs to be set aside in a relaxed, unpressurized environment to allow people to reflect upon their experiences at work (and with customers and colleagues) and to imagine even better ways of doing things, both strategically and operationally. Such reflection time should not just be the province of managers but of all employees.

## 2 Restrain from judgment

Fantasies can be wicked and if we showed no self-restraint in expressing them we might end up in gaol. Most people are therefore reluctant to divulge the exotic dreams that occasionally swirl through their minds. Furthermore, most people suspect that if they did reveal their fantasies they would be punished indirectly with statements such as "Don't be stupid!" or "You must be out of your mind!" Imagination is therefore frequently suppressed and rarely expressed. In other words we limit ourselves, fearful of the responses we might receive if we allowed ourselves unlimited expression of the images flashing through our minds.

In allowing imagination to flourish managers must encourage ideas to flow, no matter how weird and wonderful they are, and not rush into judgment. Within the boundaries of morality and law we need to refrain from exercising immediate judgment on other people's ideas, as well as loosen ourselves from our own self-restraint.

We must let loose the images employees have in their minds. We must encourage positive images of the future to flow whilst delicately flushing away the negativities. Articulation, exploration and application are the essential activities for this process, and with minimal judgmental interference. The judgment should come at the end, not at the beginning. We should not dismiss an imaginative suggestion without allowing a person to explain the idea, explore it and even experiment with its application.

## 3 Use irrelevant stimuli

Too much rationality can constrain imagination. By confining ourselves to what we deem relevant we exclude the possibility of an irrelevant idea that can spark our imagination. The conductor Benjamin Zander uses the example of Beethoven's Ninth Symphony (seemingly irrelevant) to stimulate management thinking about how to go beyond the boundaries and "live in the front row of your life." Who sits in the front row? We all know that these seats will be the last to be filled in any business meeting.

James Dyson's idea for the bagless vacuum originated when he was vacuuming his carpet at home. Housework might seem irrelevant but it sparked a fantasy in James Dyson's mind that led to a great invention around which he built a successful company. Relevance is following train tracks whilst irrelevance is exploring the vast territory of opportunity beyond the tracks and beyond the horizon of what we know. So when you pull your team together for some reflective thinking, introduce something completely irrelevant to stimulate their imaginations. Play your team your favourite pop song. Bring in a speaker to talk about climbing Mount Everest. Look under your chair and see what's there; if there's nothing there put something there. You can use it as a surprise later.

## 4  Ensure irregularity and informality

Imagination is not a regular process. It only comes to the fore when we indulge our fantasies. If we do this every five minutes we will become bored and the images will dim. We should therefore not schedule a monthly "imagination session." Far better to organize the session on a spontaneous and informal basis as and when the urge arises. One senior executive I interviewed recently took his team for a boat ride on the River Thames and entertained them to a three-hour lunch. The team had been under pressure and he wanted to let their imaginations rip. As the pressures dissolved and their positive emotions began to surface they were able to brainstorm out some suggestions for the future. "Why don't we deal with this customer this way instead of the way we have been doing in the last two years." So we'll take the customers for a three-hour lunch and boat ride on the Thames too. The key is not to have too many boat rides on the Thames. Perhaps next time it should be a walk round Virginia Water or a visit to the Imperial War Museum.

> It doesn't matter what you do to stimulate imagination as long as it is irrelevant!

## 5  Be prepared to take risks

Everything new presents a risk, especially imaginative new ideas. Unleashing the power of imagination is very risky. Not every new idea succeeds, but without any new ideas there will always be failure. This book is a huge risk, not just for me but for the publishers too. An article in *The Times* (2 June 2000) about Norman Mailer described how his highly acclaimed best selling novel *The Naked and the Dead*, published in 1948, was followed by a second novel which was trashed by the critics, as was his third novel too. "Repetition kills the soul, as Mailer is fond of repeating." Brilliant journalism! We delude ourselves that repetition will produce the same old successes, it did not for Mailer and it will not for us. Repetition and routine are risky. Similarly, stepping out of routine by introducing imaginative new ideas is also risky. We have to face up to it – life is risk, work is a risk, everything is risk. Once we accept that we are better able to deal with the risks. Creating an imaginative mind and an imaginative approach to life and work helps us deal with the risks and the daily opportunities and threats that cross our paths.

## 6 Create a stimulating environment

An imaginative environment will, by definition, stimulate the imagination. Ignorance of the environmental impact on people's minds and hearts can lead to the deadening effect of gray walls, spiritless corridors and notice boards that reek of statistical regulation and bureaucratic oppression. Flowing water and living plants will enliven the imagination. A fish, seemingly never bored with the limits of the tank, presents endless opportunities for the movement of the mind. A poster, with fine words from the guru about the merits of the soaring eagle, can inspire people to fly higher. When the walls are gray the fantasies might flow but the images are of escape – the fantasies related to work rarely see the light of reality. Too many managers dim their peoples' minds with a dull environment.

Environment is the space around us and the boundaries within which we work and imagine our work. Within this we create our own personal space. When we are crowded out, confined or cluttered up such space is eroded. Alongside the deterioration of the environment goes the deterioration of our minds and our imagination. The beauty of the countryside, of green fields, wooded glades and flowing rivers has been the inspiration for much fine art. For fine work, too, we need the inspiration of our environment, whether it be the office, the warehouse, the store or the factory.

A change of environment is equally inspirational. The imagination can often be set alight by transporting teams to country houses for a retreat into a world where fantasy merges with reality.

## 7 Be free of interruption

Interruption kills inspiration, kills imagination and kills innovative new practice. When the telephone rings the images vanish. When the boss makes incessant demands we revert to compliance rather than imagination. Stricken with constant interruption the mind loses its power to generate new ideas and focuses solely on the immediate. We easily become absorbed with the pressing priorities of today, reacting to problems with little thought and definitely with a lack of imagination. "On average I receive 120 e-mails every day" one vice-president told me recently. Another told me: "In our company anybody can check my calendar on the computer and schedule me for a meeting if I appear to be free. As a result I rarely have any free time." Our freedom, our personal space, our imagination time is interrupted by the constants demands of others and our immediate responses to them.

Successful managers free people from interruption in order to free their imaginations. The time allocated to the routine of the immediate operation and the planned delivery should be reviewed, in order to release an irregular hour or day for the sparking of imagination. The time spent on such irregular usage is incredibly valuable. Julian Richer (1995) gives his people £5 to go down the pub and brainstorm. Other companies release their people for an hour or two during off-peak periods and invite them to go shopping to spark their imaginations about what constitutes outstanding service. To get people to work better you must first stop them working.

## 8  Develop skills in imagination and application

Imagination requires two skills. First, the skill to create the fantasy and drag the pertinent image from it. Second, the skill to bring the image to life. The first skill is latent in most humans yet rarely practised. For a company to create the conditions for imaginative improvements it must help people develop their skills in imagination. There is nothing magic in this development process. It is simply a matter of doing it. It is simply a matter of allowing our imaginations to let rip, with the aid of a suitable stimulus, and then picking up those ideas that are going to lead to genuine improvements and implementing them. A method for stimulating imagination is provided below and will help people develop their skills. These skills can be applied to everyday behavior and interactions with colleagues and customers. They can also be applied to the strategic development of the business. The opportunities for the application of these skills are boundless.

## 9  Work hard and practice

Regrettably it is not enough to have wonderful skills in imagination. To bring the images to life requires immense skill, hard work and practice. The saying "Achievement is 1 per cent inspiration and 99 per cent perspiration" is as true today as it ever was. As with any skill, an essential condition for applying it imaginatively is hard work and practice. Unleashing the imagination to yield creative ideas will not lead to improvements unless an excessive amount of phyical and emotional energy is deployed in realizing those ideas. The difference between one competitor and another is not just the power of imagination but the power with which imagination is realized to achieve a standard of product or service which is better than the rest. The difference between a gold and silver medal in the Olympics might be a hundredth of a second. The minute "hair's breadth" difference is everything, with the result, like the title of the song by ABBA "The winner takes all." The scarcely measurable fine difference is a product not only of imagination but of hard work and practice. To be a hundredth of a second ahead of a competitor and win everything requires a phenomenal amount of energy. It is in fact an extension of Pareto's 80:20 law (Fig. 9.3), in which the first 20 per cent of effort produces the first 80 per cent of result, whilst the last 80 per cent of effort produces the final 20 per cent of result.

> To bring the images to life requires immense skill, hard work and practice

Given an equal amount of luck, the difference between success and failure can often be a small fraction created by a big number of units of imagination and energy. Pavarotti once said: "Others practise ten times to be good, I practise one hundred times to be even better." Valery Gergiev will make the orchestra repeat something 25 times to achieve the quality he requires. These top performers have an image in their minds of the very best and will then not be satisfied until they achieve it. As Andrew Billen (2000) wrote: "Valery Gergiev, the brilliant, difficult, infinitely driven artistic director of the Kirov in St Petersburg has, I suspect, not merely a better version of Tchaikovsky's *Sleeping Beauty* going on in his head, but a perfect one."

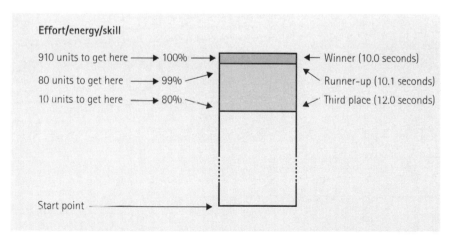

**Fig 9.3**

Beating the competition

It is that image of perfection we need to create in our heads and move towards. It might be a fantasy, but to realize that image of perfect quality requires an immense amount of hard work and practice. Whilst routine will never yield such perfection, the infinitesimal improvements created by frequent practice will lead to it. Practice, practice and practice enables us to push back the boundaries of our art to realize the imaginative ideas of perfection we have in our heads. Business management is an art and we have to work hard at practising it, to improve the way we deal with customers and colleagues, to improve the way we make improvements, to improve the way we do business. To perfect a greeting we have to practise it. To perfect a simple "thank you" we have to practise it. We practise it by having an image in our minds of the perfect greeting and the perfect "thank you."

The model given earlier in this chapter (Fig. 9.1) can thus be developed to incorporate the key step of hard work and practice in developing an imaginative idea for an improvement (*see* Fig. 9.4).

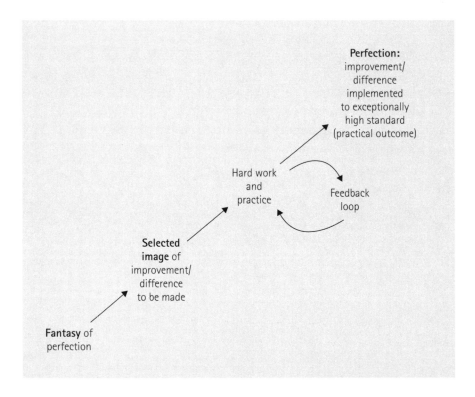

**Fig 9.4**

Adding hard work and practice to an imaginative idea

The word "improvement" has to be qualified here. It can indeed relate to any future practical outcome that is better than the current state. However, "improvement" has a judgmental implication that something will be "better." Imagination does not just relate to making something better. It can also relate to making a difference or creating something new (*see* Fig. 9.5).

In business we should not therefore confine ourselves solely to imagining improvements but also to imagining and bringing into reality aspects of our business that are either different or new. Customers are not necessarily looking for improvements to your products and services, but what they will definitely be attracted to is something that is different or new. That is the "stimulus for customers" mentioned in the next chapter. When Starbucks bring out a "Rhumba Frappucino" many people will want to try it as an alternative to iced coffee and for the stimulus of a new taste experience. However, the process of bringing such ideas to fruition requires hard work. "They varied the ingredients," wrote Howard Schultz (1997). "They lengthened the blending time from 10 to 25 seconds. They changed the ratio of ice to liquid. They tasted all the competing products. They got feedback from customers."

> Nothing succeeds without a combination of imagination and hard work

The idea for the Frappucino was almost rejected from the start:

Many entrepreneurs fall into a trap. They are so captivated by their own vision that when an employee comes up with an idea, especially one that doesn't seem to fit the original vision, they are tempted to quash it. I almost did the same for one of Starbucks' most successful products, the icy blend of dark-roasted coffee and milk that we call Frappucino.

Ultimately nothing succeeds without a combination of imagination and hard work.

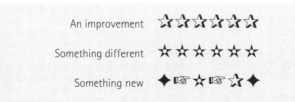

Fig 9.5

The products of imagination

# Seven steps to stimulate your imagination

There are seven critical steps for stimulating the imagination, whether it be your own or that of your team.

## 1 Create the conditions for imagination

The first step is to create a set of conditions that are ripe for imagination. These have been explained in the previous section of this chapter:

1 Create a relaxing environment.

2 Restrain from judgment.

3 Use irrelevant stimuli.

4 Ensure irregularity and informality.

5 Be prepared to take risks.

6 Create a stimulating environment.

7 Be free of interruption.

8 Develop skills in imagination and application.

9 Work hard and practise

## 2 Declare your aspiration

Imagination is best focused on your aspiration. What do you really aspire to at work (or at home)? If your aspiration is to marry the most beautiful person in the world then you can allow your fantasy to run riot with a wide range of fascinating images of this person. If your aspiration is to inject some excitement into your work situation and create a "buzz" for your team and for your customers, then again you can create a fantasy around this. Here are some aspirations declared to me by people who were interviewed as part of this research:

- To work with a team where everyone loves what they do.
- To have customers frequently tell us that our service is wonderful.
- To be appreciated for all the hard work we put in.
- To go home on a Friday evening feeling we have made a difference to the lives of our customers.
- To get rid of all the internal politics and negativity that abound here.

## 3 Stimulate your imagination

Keeping the aspiration in mind, stimulate your imagination to create a fantasy in which your aspirations have been realized. Try to capture as many images from this fantasy as possible by shouting them out and tape-recording them or have someone write them on a flip-chart. Here is a typical fantasy that relates to one of the above-stated aspirations – to work with a team where everyone loves what they do:

- Everyone greets each other in the morning with two kisses on the cheek.
- We have a camera at the entrance that can detect and count smiles using a digitial display.
- We create a "love board" on which we put post-it notes of the things other people do that we love.
- We have a weekly "love and hate" session in which we honestly express our feelings about things we have loved and hated at work this week.
- Our bosses notices all the great things we do.
- Something new happens every day.
- Something special happens every day.
- Nobody ever says anything nasty about anything or anyone.
- We tell our customers we love them.
- We tell our colleagues we love them.
- We tell our bosses we love them.
- Our boss tells us he/she loves us.
- We serve our customers with love.

If necessary you might require a second "pass" at this step to "color in" some of these images. For example if someone says "Something special happens every day" you will need to come up with some practical examples of this and what you mean by "special."

## 4 Select the image

Having created and recorded the fantasy the next step is to select one or more images from it that your gut instinct tells you can be put into practice. This might be all of the images you have captured or just one of them. In the above fantasy the camera may not be possible but the "love board" is a possible candidate for selection. It is best just to select one image from the fantasy to begin with and pursue this to reality before returning to the fantasy, possibly revising it and then selecting other images.

## 5 Validate the image

It is worth spending some time reflecting on the image selected and validating it against the following criteria:

- Is it new (or different or an improvement)?
- Will it be acceptable to most of our customers and colleagues?
- Will it help our business and /or the way we work?
- How do we really feel about it? (Do we really mean it?)
- What are the risks involved?
- Do we have the skills, the energy, the time (and if appropriate the money) to put it into practice?

## 6 Plan the practice

What practical steps do we now need to take to convert the selected image into a practical reality? This might involved changes in behavior, in thinking and attitude, as well as more mechanical steps such as bringing about changes to our procedures, environment and equipment. Here is a hypothetical plan:

- Within one week we will think more about where best to site the "love board." Paul will check this out with various people and make the final decision.
- Paul will also consult Building Services Department as to the various practical options (size, style, cost etc.).
- We will start the process immediately by sending each other "love notes," either in writing or by e-mail. For example "I just loved the way you handled that recent situation with XYZ…"
- As soon as the board is up we will start posting "love notices" on it.
- We agree to abide by the following simple rules:
  - love notices will be simple with just a few words;
  - love notices will be colorful;
  - love notices will be genuine;
  - love notices will be work related;

- love notices will always be signed by the author and dated;
- love notices will not be the vehicle for any private romances;
- love notices will never embarrass (always respecting a person's dignity).

## 7 Undertake an "imaginative review"

Within a month or two of the imaginative idea being implemented then the team should undertake an "imaginative review" during which they reflect on their experiences and the extent to which the practical outcome aligns with the original aspiration. If the idea does not work out, nobody should be hurt if it is dropped. The ebb and flow of imagination and practice will be part of the learning experience. The review can then go on to develop the previous fantasy and select further images for practical implementation. Such reviews should never be bureaucratic or formal. They should not rely on a boring set of minutes of the last meeting. The process for stimulating imagination should be stimulating in itself.

# Creating fantastic images of the future

In summary, reality is no more than a set of pictures in our minds. Divorced from the present reality of what we see and hear at this moment we are left with nothing but pictures of the past and of the future. The pictures of the past, our memories, rapidly become distorted and grow fuzzy with age. Even so they are invaluable as stimuli for creating our fantasies of the future. However, it is the stimulus of our pictures of the future – of our imagination – that carry us forward.

> The secret of success in business management is to concentrate on the future and to create fantastic images of it

The secret of success in business management is not therefore to concentrate too much on the current picture but on the future and to create fantastic images of it. If Steve Jobs had not had such a fantastic image of the future back in 1982 I would not be sitting writing this on my PC today. Speaking back in 1982 he said: "What we're doing has never been done before ... My dream is that every person in the world will have their own Apple computer" (Sculley, 1987). His dream almost came true; whilst not everyone has a computer made by Apple, the pioneering work done by Steve

Jobs and Steve Wozniak 20 or 30 years ago was a sufficient stimulus to ensure the accessability of computers to millions of people today.

Steve Jobs' dream back in the 1970s was high level. At a lower level we can all have daily dreams of a different tomorrow, of a better way of relating to people, of a different way of conducting our business, of a new range of exciting products and service. One final example of this is a story told by Richard Fannon, General Manager of Lainston House, a charming historic hotel in the depths of the Hampshire countryside in the UK. One of his cleaners, Valerie, always seemed to get behind with her cleaning schedule, never getting her work done on time. The main reason for this was she was always chatting to guests who passed her by and sometimes these conversations would go on for a long time. Rather than discipline her for poor performance Richard Fannon decided to capitalize on her strengths. He relieved her of her cleaning duties and gave her a roving remit to chat to guests, to meet and greet them, to help them, to keep an eye on them and help them wherever possible. The guests loved it and returned time and time again. Valerie excels at the work and has developed a charm which enraptures guests. "Valerie takes real pleasure in other people's happiness" Richard Fannon says, "and this is an attribute we like to see in all our staff."

When you have a fantasy of happy guests then you can create an image of the type of staff who will make them happy. As soon as you create that image in your mind you will discover and develop the Valeries of this world. This is the stimulus for customers and the subject of the next chapter.

# 10

# A stimulus
# for customers

The motivation of a customer to buy is not just a function of
the price and specification nor a function of a customer's direct
needs and wants. It is also a function of the stimulus provided
by the total purchasing experience.

The world of commerce is built around three motivational needs: first,
subsistence and survival; second, the stimulus of experiencing or possessing
something different or new; and third, the way we identify ourselves with
certain groups or clubs.

## The customer's need for a stimulus

If the world of commerce was built solely on meeting our needs for survival
and subsistence there would be little need for the world of commerce. As
soon as we think we have secured our future we seek exposure to the various
clusters of stimuli in order to obtain new experiences. The stimuli we seek
might relate to discovery, learning, diversion, altruism, change, freedom or
aspiration. The need for a stimulus creates a world of activity for activity's
sake and of purchase for purchasing's sake. We travel when we need not
travel and we buy things we never use, let alone need. To discover the
evidence, clear out the garage, empty the loft and get rid of the junk! It is all

there – the thousand photographs we never look at, the hundred books we will never read again, the magazines we have forgotten about, the ornaments we have discarded and the many tools we never use. There you will find the historical remains of our need for a new stimulus, for a new camera, for a new book, for a new tool, for something fresh in our lives, for something which in most cases went stale the following day.

> The need for a stimulus creates a world of activity for activity's sake and of purchase for purchasing's sake

## The customer's club

When a purchase is not linked to survival and subsistence what stimulates customers to buy is not only the prospect of something new or different but also the need to reinforce our association with the "club." The process of purchase stimulates the mind and helps us reinforce our individual identities; it provides us with essential life-stores of experiences and memories, which in turn stimulate our social relationships in the club. The paradox is that in defining ourselves through the stimulus of purchase we also attempt to define the clubs to which we wish to belong, whether those clubs be families, peer groups, neighborhood communities, sports teams, institutions, professional bodies, our sections at work or loose affiliations with the organizations we support.

The conflict with which we frequently toy is the need to be unique and the need to conform – the need to dress differently and the need to wear uniforms. The latest fashion can be both a differentiator and a uniform. The creative stimulus through which we establish an individual identity is often at war with the social stimulus that motivates us to belong to the club.

The world of commerce provides the essential stimuli for all three elements of motivation: the struggle to survive, the struggle to define ourselves and the struggle to join and remain members of certain social groups (or what I call clubs). To accomplish each of these we need a stimulus to trigger the essential energies for life maintenance, self-definition and socialization. The world of commerce provides such stimuli and as customers we constantly seek to respond to thcm.

I do not belong to the club whose members have tattoos on their arms, wear rings in their ears and consume vast amounts of ale. Instead I belong to the club that wears ties, drinks designer coffees, takes moderates exercise but still puts on weight.

## Surviving without the stimulus to buy

Recently I saw a rack of ties as I walked through a department store en route to a coffee shop to purchase a caffe latte I didn't need (at least for nutritional reasons). Instinctively I started looking at these ties and fingering one or two. An assistant approached me and without too much further thought I bought the tie that attracted me most. I didn't need the tie. I have over 30 ties back home. Perhaps I was rewarding myself, perhaps I wanted to look different for the seminar I was giving the following day, perhaps I was bored and was just succumbing to that irrepressible but irritating urge to buy something. I could have survived without the tie and without the caffe latte. In fact I could survive without 90 per cent of the things I purchase. I could survive without most of the telephone calls I make (although one or two are essential). I could survive without the mineral water I drink and without the exotic fruits and fancy cereals I like to have for breakfast. I could survive without such a large house and I could survive without the expensive chair I am sitting in right at this moment. It is arguable whether I could survive without my PC and laptop, although I could just about survive without the internet – I have done so for most of my life. In fact most people in history have survived without any of the above.

> Most people in history have survived without most of the items we consider essential today

## The product is often less important than the purchase experience

In many cases the act of purchase is as important as the product purchased. The act of purchase is the stimulus rather than the product itself. It is the stimulus of selection, of transaction, of acquisition, of possession, of display, and then of utilization. These acts of purchase, in addition to the product acquired, are all essential to the way we define ourselves in relation to others. In my office I have 12 small sculptures – some wooden, some in stone, some metallic – the last being purchased when a beautiful Russian sculpture took my eye in an art gallery in Eton. The visit to the gallery, meetings some friends there, the beautiful exhibits and the unintended purchase all combined to create a stimulating experience far superior to any experience I could have gained from making the same purchase by mail order or through the internet.

Now I have made the purchase of this and other small sculptures I am provided with additional fleeting visual stimuli as I sit in my office and write.

But the stimulus is greater than that. If my shelves were bare and there was nothing to adorn my walls then I would have no such stimulus. Nor would the guests who visit me here. They are part of my club and as such I want them to experience the same visual stimuli when I show them around. If my walls were bare I would not have these guests. I would have different guests and they would be part of a different club. Each *object d'art* provides a stimulus – as does the piano playing of Nelson Freire to which I am listening at the moment. My family (who are at the heart of my club) provide me with a stimulus in the same way that I attempt to provide it for them. It is the stimulus of conversation – of staying up late to discuss those fascinating things that I have forgotten by the morning. Perhaps it is Mozart, perhaps it is the situation in Venezuela, perhaps it is the merits of drinking mineral water, perhaps it is what we plan to do tomorrow, perhaps it is the eccentricities of some of our friends, perhaps it is the news. The world of commerce provides the stimulus – the Mozart, the travel opportunity, the mineral water, the entertainment, the television and, believe it or not, the opportunity to extend the club to include new friends. Without the world of commerce our walls would be bare and we would talk only of tomorrow's meal and the people we know in the village. Our conversation would be different and so would our friends.

## The choice is the stimulus

Why do I prefer my tea in this mug and not that one? Why do I prefer this casual shirt and rarely wear that one? Why do I prefer this newspaper to that one? Why do I like to use this pen and not that one? Will any old pen do? Does it really matter? If the answer is 'No' then the world of commerce would disappear. The choice is the stimulus and modern business provides that choice.

What stimulates me is to discover why one person chooses to do this and another chooses to do that, why one person chooses to rate a piece of my work three out of five and another person chooses to rate the same piece five out of five, why one person chooses to watch football and another basketball, why one person likes Madonna and another prefers Mozart, why one person likes to talk and another likes to listen, why one person likes television soap whilst another (me!) rarely watches television, why one person belongs to this club and another to that.

# The increasing range of stimuli

Our individual uniqueness as humans demands a unique stimulus. If we all ate the same type of bread and drank the same type of water we would all be the same. What differentiates us is our responses to the ever increasing range of stimuli available to us. The greater the number of stimuli available to us the greater the possibilities we have for defining ourselves. Without such stimuli life would be grey and we would all seem alike. But the paradox is that at times we want to be alike whilst at the same time wanting to be different. We want to belong and we want to be apart.

The world of commerce provides the essential stimuli to resolve that paradox – it enables us to create the differentiators that separate us from others whilst at the same time as providing the uniform badges that show that we belong. We dress up our lives with a combination of differentiators and badges that display the boundaries between our individuality and our allegiances. We might visit the same restaurants as our friends and take the same types of vacations as they do. We might want to be the same in many ways, mixing in their circle and participating in shared interests. But we also want to be different. We want to be accepted for what we are, not as replicas of what they are. We create this individual uniqueness through nuances of personal differences, through the unique stories we tell based on the unique experiences we have and through our unique behaviors and attitudes.

> We need to keep varying the stimuli, creating new sets of stimulating experiences for our customers

## Differentiators and unifiers

The world of commerce facilitates the balancing act of creating both differentiating and unifying experiences.

The clubs, the groups, the institutions, the professions, the villages, the companies, the communities, the neighborhoods ebb and flow like giant amoebae. Sometimes we are part of them and sometimes we are apart from them. We subscribe to the latest club fashion and then, when everybody does, stop subscribing and move on to other niches that will set us apart in the eyes of others. We will shop here and then start shopping there. We will buy this today and that tomorrow. It will never be the same. Even our dogs and cats have to be tempted with new pet foods – even they cannot stomach the same can of compressed meat every day. To succeed in providing the differentiators and unifiers we thus need to keep varying the stimuli, creating new sets of stimulating experiences for our customers.

Our club is the "market segment" that commercial companies seek to target, but that market is never static. We move from one market to another as we seek to belong and then set ourselves apart in the lifelong process of defining ourselves. My 86-year-old mother is now in the great-grand-mothers' club and I have recently joined the grandfathers' club. The world of commerce has thus put me into a different market. However, I can move away from it if I wish, defining myself as young in thought. So I still buy pop music even though I am not in that market segment.

The delicate balance between sameness and differentiation extends to our lives at work. When everyone does the same thing and every day is the same work becomes drudgery and we lose our identities and emulate robots. The monotony deadens the mind and boredom becomes a disease that yields to low performance. Few people can become lost in their thoughts for eight hours a day as their hands repeat the same tasks 80 times an hour.

## Customers and the stimulus of discovery

Shopping provides an escape. It stimulates our fantasies from which we choose our experiences. These in turn provide the stories back at the club. The dream is of a new experience, of a discovery. We discover a price, we discover a different product, we discover a new way. The discovery is the stimulus that creates the experience. In the club we exchange stories about our various experiences: "I really got a bargain with those shoes I bought at …" or "I'd never go back there again after the way they treated me." In this way we constantly push back the boundaries of our experience and keep ourselves alive with each fresh discovery. Without it we would be brain-dead.

### Once there was salad cream

Once there was salad cream and it served many purposes. At home in the 1950s we spread salad cream on the cheese in our sandwiches and we had it with cold ham and chips. We even had it with salads. Now there is little salad cream to be found. Instead we find mayonnaises and relishes of all descriptions, with or without avocado, with or without fresh ingredients, with or without herbs, with or without spices, with or without additives good or bad. When there was only salad cream to be found then salad cream was the stimulus to enliven a cheese sandwich or an egg salad. But it was not enough. The stimulus was temporary. The stimulus of salad cream had to be replaced with the stimulus of a much wider range of salad dressings. People needed the stimulus of new experiences so they could tell new stories to the people at the club. So they started talking about avocado, garlic, chillis, fresh ingredients, organic produce and other things they had never talked about before.

Once there was bread. It was a loaf of bread and at best there were three variations of it. Now there are one hundred types of bread ranging from pita, to focaccia to ciabatta, to naan, to rye, to oatmeal, to wholegrain, to onion bread, to cheese bread, to tomato bread and to whatever the world of commerce creates next to stimulate our interest.

Once there was water – tap water. It was pure and simple. Now the shelves of our supermarkets are stocked with at least 40 different types of bottled water. There used not to be bottled water, unless we went for long-distance rides on our bicycles, and then it was tap water in plastic bottles.

Once there was one film showing at the local cinema. Now there are 20. There is a film for everyone. Before it was just a film for one or two of us.

Once there were airports and you checked in, went through immigration and then waited patiently to be called to a gate where you waited patiently again. At best there was a little place at which you could buy coffee or purchase a magazine. Today airports like Heathrow, Dubai and Changi are saturated with stimuli to alleviate the potential boredom of passengers. Few people if any need to buy a shirt at an airport, let alone purchase most of the items at the hundreds of retail outlets that now make airports so fascinating. Who needs Mickey Mouse or the Disney Store at an airport? The answer is that we all do if we define our desire for stimuli as a need. Each retail outlet at an airport provides a stimulus for the eye and for the touch ("Just feel this silk scarf – and I love the color too!" or "Do you like this leather handbag? It's rather unusual!"). The retail outlets at airports stimulate our fantasies from which, with a swift swipe of our credit card, we select images for conversion into reality.

Through travel we are often indulging our fantasies of exotic foreign lands where things are far better than the drabness of our own environment back home. It is, of course, a fantasy exploited by the world of commerce with its shiny images and sexy advertisements. So we select the image we desire,

**The world of commerce is the world of the stimulus**

spend the money we don't have, and for a moment attempt to create the reality we imagine. Money helps and the world of commerce is there to help us. Fortunately, the reality is sometimes exceptionally good. The journey to

Hong Kong, the new scarf, the new leather handbag and the experiences we soak up en route really make us feel good, and it's even better when we get back home and can tell everyone about it. Regrettably, the reality is occasionally far divorced from the fantasy.

The world of commerce is the world of the stimulus. It offers us an ever increasing range of products and services which can stimulate the new experiences we are desperate for. It might be the experience of seat-back videos on trains as they now have in Hong Kong on the service between downtown Kowloon and the new Chep Lap Kok airport, or it might be the fashion show at the local department store. It might be the stimulus of travel or the stimulus of the internet or a stimulus as yet unknown. The more stimuli we offer the more people buy and the more our economies grow. Prosperity is directly proportionate to the variety of stimuli on offer to a populace.

## The secret of the stimulus factor

The secret therefore is to keep stimulating customers with the prospect of new experiences. It is these new experiences that enable people to differentiate themselves from others as well affiliate themselves with others. Without any such experiences we would be confined to our villages, subsist on seasonal produce and the only travel we would know would be a two-hour walk to a neighboring village.

Thus the challenge is continually to create new stimuli for customers so that they have the potential of enjoying new experiences and feeling good as a result. It is not that bulk standard salad cream is any worse than the latest garlic mayonnaise, it is just that customers like to have their tongues stimulated by enticing new taste experiences. The same applies to all our physical senses as well as to our emotions, intellects and spirits. They all need different or new experiences from time to time to keep them alive and fresh. Thus the routine experience of seeing a film at the cinema has to be enhanced with the first-class experience of a premier screen with a lounge facility and free popcorn. The supermarket, sensitive to the lack of stimulus in tap water, seeks to relieve our monotony by offering us new experiences with a wide range of mineral waters, often with fruity hints of this and herbal traces of that. To stimulate us further they even redesign the bottles and put on new-style caps for ease of drinking.

> The secret is to keep stimulating customers with the prospect of new experiences

## Not necessarily better but different

The new stimulus is not necessarily better than before but it definitely offers a different or new experience. Thus it is arguable whether mineral water is better for you than tap water. However, it definitely offers a different experience in terms of purchase, display and possibly consumption. Consumers are desperate for such differences as it helps them define themselves in terms of their own individual identities, as well as the clubs to which they belong. In my club people are considered eccentric if they ask for tap water. They prefer the stimulus of a nice-looking bottle of mineral water together with an original label. My late father was in the club that never drank mineral water – it was beyond his comprehension. However, he did once yield to a cappuccino after years of white coffee consumption and this provided him with a stimulus. He certainly talked about it long afterwards and was well able to pronounce the word incorrectly: "We had a really good cappatuna at that place in London!"

In practical terms this means that you must constantly seek to create something new or different to stimulate your customers. This could be new ways of serving them or new products with which to entice them. It might mean doing business with them in a different way. Even the staple requirements for maintaining life (such as bread, rice or potato) have to be dressed up with new recipes and packaging to stimulate new experiences.

# Experimenting with new stimuli

To create an effective stimulus for customers requires continuous experimentation, whether it be with new displays, new products or new pricing regimes. However, the challenge is not solely with displays, products and prices. It also relates to the soft side of service and finding new behaviors that stimulate the interest of customers and their desire to have relationships with your company. It might mean stepping outside the counter when traditionally you have stayed behind it. It might mean informing your customers of things you have never informed them of before. It might mean showing them the kitchen of your restaurant or giving them a complimentary drink when they least expect it. It might just mean taking a greater interest in your customers than you have previously done, asking them questions you never thought of asking them before. It probably means transcending many of the routines and varying each interaction with each customer as much as possible. Tell a story, invite a story, pass a comment, invite a comment, make a joke, make a compliment or just aim to make your customers happier than before.

The only thing it does not mean is staying the same as before. Your business has to move on if it is to continue stimulating the interest of your customers. This does not mean ditching the traditional things your customers value. Tradition is evolutionary and never static. You can keep tradition but you have to build on it. Even tradition can be repackaged to provide a fresh stimulus.

## The daily challenge of the stimulus factor

Daily you should challenge yourselves. What's new for my customers? How can I keep my relationship with them alive and fresh? What stimulus can I provide for them to enhance their experience of life? Change the music, change the décor, change the way people work, change the style of invitation, change the introduction, change the product specification. Change for change's sake! Never assume that what your customers liked yesterday is what they will like tomorrow. As the world moves on it is a fine judgment as to what to keep for your customers and what to discard. It will depend on relationships, quality and price – each of these will need to be stimulated from time to time. In their pursuit of efficiency too many organizations today are eroding their relationships with customers. They are becoming remote from customers at a time when many still desire the stimulus of personal contact.

The same applies to quality. I am reminded of the following quote from Queen Elizabeth I who, back in the sixteenth century said: "I take a bath once a month, whether I need it or not." This was not good news for bathmakers. But quality, and therefore the quality of life, is a mindset with boundaries that can forever be pushed back. It might be the quality of the visual design, or the reliability, or the functionality, or the quality of the service supporting the product. In June 2000 a new bridge was opened across the River Thames, which had received many accolades for the quality of its design. The only trouble was that it wobbled in the wind and some people stumbled and fell as they crossed it. One person commented: "It was a terrible experience." Engineers said that the bridge would have to undergo extensive remedial works, possibily incorporating shock absorbers. Quality can always be improved, even the latest quality designs. Customers are stimulated by high quality and with increasing affluence will seek more of it as they seek to enhance the quality of their lives. Yet this stimulus has to be counterbalanced by the stimulus of price, by the perception of value for money and by a feel-good factor associated with obtaining a bargain. People are stimulated by a bargain and therefore a "win."

## The stimulus of winning

Successful business people know that the customer must always win. The art is to stimulate that feeling of winning: of obtaining a great bargain, of completing a favorable deal, of obtaining immense value for money, of receiving something extra – over and above that expected. It might be the complimentary cup of coffee, or the rounding down of a price, or the extra

> Successful business people know that the customer must always win

item thrown in as a gift, or the additional time for which no charge is made. It might be waiving the rules in order to give a customer the benefit of the doubt. It might be a flower in a buttonhole or a candy for the kids. It might be one of a thousand different stimuli, but if each customer walks out saying "I've won, I've had a great experience" then the stimulus will have been effective and the business will be successful. The stimulus comes from doing positive things for customers – from surprising them with unexpected delights and creating for them experiences that make them happy to be alive.

I like to make my clients feel good. So when they ask for a discount I often give them one. I want them to feel good about negotiating me down to a lower price. There is a line I draw in my mind and the line varies according to the extent I like the customer and want to work for them. In other words, I like to inject a positive emotion into my relationships with customers – I want them to feel good as a result of the positive steps I take. If I can make them happy by letting them bargain me down I let them do so. Why argue about money all the time? Let the customer win! Let the customer win some money from you!

### Count the cost of guarding the pennies

Whatever your business, whether it be large or small, there are daily opportunities to stimulate the goodwill of your customers. If you count the cost in terms of pennies and the time in terms of minutes you will not find these opportunities, but if you create opportunities to give your customers additional value and extra time then you will discover a great dividend downstream.

It is the extra pennies and the extra minutes that you give away that create the essential stimuli for excellent customer relations. Conversely it is the pennies you save and the time you deny customers that destroy such relationships. If you think only in terms of money and time then your customer will too and you will fight it out with them on that basis. With increasing choice, customers can always deny you their time and money. However, if you think in terms of "gifts" then your customers will give you their business. But they have to be genuine gifts – not only of money and time but of genuine interest in the customer's well-being.

## The ideal gift for a customer

The ideal gift comes from the heart – it is the essential stimulus of positive emotion that should accompany every interaction with a customer in attempting to give them what they require, and more.

At my local newspaper shop recently an old lady in front of me was purchasing a magazine. She groped in her handbag before realizing she had left her purse on the mantelpiece at home. "Don't worry, Mrs Smith," said Janet behind the counter. "Take the magazine and pay me the next time you come in." It was the gift of understanding and trust – a vital stimulus to any relationship.

> If you think in terms of "gifts" then your customers will give you their business

Recently I was in the Far East having a working dinner with a client in a Korean restaurant. We had arrived early when the restaurant was empty and we spread our papers out across the table to work as we dined. Half-an-hour later a party of six men arrived and sat at the table behind us. They started talking and joking rather noisily. As the noise continued our waitress became concerned for us. She suggested we move to a quieter area at the other end of the restaurant. We did so. Hers was a gift of concern and of care. For her the noise was the stimulus for her to act and to show us how much she valued our custom. She wanted us to be happy and therefore she was happy for us to move. We will go back.

# Stimulating your relationships with customers

Every day, every week, every year there are opportunities to stimulate your relationships with customers. If you allow your customers to be processed by way of routine and procedure then there will be no stimulus excepting the negative possibility that a customer might defect. When a relationship is not stimulated, the energy seeps out of it and eventually people feel bad. The secret is to inject fresh energy into each relationship with a customer in order to keep it alive.

Use the following checklist to challenge your own actions relating to customers as well as to those of your team. Some of these checks should be done on a daily basis.

## 1  New things – What new things have you done for your customers recently?

As soon as you step beyond routine, habit and procedure you are in new territory. You will find yourself doing "new things" or "different things" to create even more positive experiences for your customers. Therefore challenge yourself and your team to identify at least one new thing that has been done or initiated recently for customers. It does not matter whether this new thing is big or small – magnitude is irrelevant. The critical thing is to create some new experience for your customers.

## 2  Gifts – What extra things did you give your customers today?

This is essential. Every day you *must* give something extra to your customers. When you drive home you must be able to answer the question: "What extra things did I give my customers today over and above their expectations of dealing with me?"

The concept of "gifts" for customers is not new. However the key to giving is to do it from the heart – make it spontaneous and make it personal. Routine gifts sent in an impersonal manner are far less effective. Gifts should not be confined to external customers but also extended to internal customers and colleagues. Gifts are as equally applicable to retail situations as to business-to-business interactions. The gifts should also be small, not necessarily of any financial value and should never be presented in such a way that they will be misconstrued as (dare I say it) bribery or corruption.

## 3 Personal interest – Did you take a genuine interest in some of your customers today?

Most of us are stimulated by the interest shown in us by others. The simplest thing you can do for customers is take an interest in them – not necessarily in the products and services they might potentially purchase, but in them as human beings.

Many front-line people shy away from this, not confident of the approach and fearful of an adverse reaction if they pry into people's lives. The secret is to initiate the relationship with a potentially new customer with the stimulus of an innocuous question. As soon as a relationship is established it can then be extended with the stimulus of a fresh set of questions which take a further interest in the customer. The key is to probe gently with polite questions, thus push back the boundaries of our knowledge and understanding about each customer. The more we know about customers the better position we will be in to help meet their requirements.

Remember that all relationships start with the briefest of encounters.

## 4 Lessons – What have you learnt recently about improving your approach to customers?

We delude ourselves that we know it all, yet at the same time we all know that we have much to learn. The challenge is to focus on the lessons. Every day presents a lesson, especially in the way we relate to customers and colleagues. Nick Clayton, General Manager of the Ritz Carlton Hotel, Singapore, uses the company's "credo" and 20 "basics" to challenge everyday practice and learn how to improve it. The "credo" and 20 "basics" represent an ideal model of how to behave in relation to customers.

> Every day presents a lesson, especially in the way we relate to customers and colleagues

Lessons are best learnt when we have an ideal model in our mind of how we should relate to customers. The clearer that ideal, the more effective it is as an aspirational stimulus for exposing the gaps between current and ideal practice. The gaps present the learning opportunities. We can learn from other people and other organizations (and ourselves) and thus push back the boundaries of our "ideal model."

Recently I learnt that when I was speaking to an audience I tended to make eye contact with the people on the right-hand side but rarely with the people on the left-hand side. This was because I was standing to the left of the projector and therefore at a slight angle to the audience. Part of the "ideal model" for a speaker is to have eye contact with that audience. The feedback from a member of the audience (my customers) was invaluable.

What did you learn today?

## 5 Reflection time (daily) – How much time did you spend today on reflecting on how you can do things better for your customers or in a new or different way?

At the end of the day ask yourself how much time you dedicated today to reflect on ways of doing things differently or better for your customers. Unless you can specify a period during the day when this happened then the probability is that it did not happen. It is essential that you can identify at least five minutes every day when you reflect on your experiences with customers and colleagues and explored ways of doing things differently.

Use this reflection time to examine the interactions you and your team have with your customers. Try to focus on three things:

- What did you do today that your customers really liked?
- What did you do today that your customers disliked?
- What did you do in your relationships with customers that was rather ordinary?

Be prepared to face some painful truths. It is not enough to reflect on successes. An essential stimulus comes from the things we do badly and which our customers dislike – these might be as simple as an indifferent stare, a failure to ring back or an abrupt tone on the telephone.

## 6 Reflection time (strategic) – How much time did you spend during the last six months reflecting on how you can do things better for your customers or in a new or different way?

Whilst you can reflect daily on how to do things differently to stimulate the interest of your customers it is also important to take a day off every six months to reflect on the strategic opportunities for providing your customers with new or better experiences. It is at these off-sites or retreats that an opportunity should be seized to create mental images about the product range or the services your company or team provides. Everything within your area that has an impact on customers should be reviewed, whether it be window displays, pricing policies, product range or market strategies. The key is to reflect and "feel." You can apply logic later, but initially it is important to use this strategic reflection time to stimulate mental pictures of improvements which you feel will have a substantial impact on customers.

## 7 A stimulus for customers – How have you stimulated your customers recently?

The ultimate test stems from the previous six checks and depends on your answers to the following questions:

- Have you got into a rut with your customers?
- Are you taking them for granted?
- Are you neglecting your customers?

Or:

- Have you recently provided them with a stimulating experiences (new, different, better) which they really like?
- Do you have further new stimuli in mind to keep your relationships with customers fresh?
- Are you experimenting enough and taking sufficient risks in apply the stimulus factor?

These seven stimulus checks can in fact be applied to all the relationships you enjoy (and perhaps don't enjoy!) in your life and at work. The word "customer" is merely a label for a certain type of human being and the checks of:

1 Doing new things
2 Giving extra
3 Taking a personal interest
4 Learning to make improvements
5 Reflecting daily on doing things better or differently
6 Reflecting strategically
7 Stimulating others

are equally applicable to your employees, your employers, your friends, your family and yourself. In fact these seven checks are the ultimate test for putting "the stimulus factor" to work.

# References

Baum, L. Frank (1900) *The Wizard of Oz*, Penguin Books 1995.

Beer, Michael and Nohria, Nitin (2000) "Cracking the code of change," *Harvard Business Review*, May–June.

Bethune, Gordon (1998) *From Worst to First*, John Wiley.

Billen, Andrew (2000) in *The Evening Standard*, 7 June.

Branson, Richard (1998) *Losing My Virginity*, Virgin Publishing.

Brown, Wilfred (1960) *Exploration in Management*, Heinemann.

Bullimore, Tony (1997) *Saved*, Little, Brown & Co.

Chang, Jung (1991) *Wild Swans*, HarperCollins.

Chu, Ching-Ning (1995) *Thick Face, Black Heart*, Nicholas Brealey Publishing.

Coombs, Nigel (2000) "Flying solo," *Director Journal*, April.

Dawkins, Richard (1996) *Climbing Mount Improbable*, W. W. Norton & Co.

Drucker, Peter F. (1967) *The Effective Executive*, London: Heinemann.

Edwardes, Michael (1984) *Back From the Brink*, Collins.

Emerson, Ralph Waldo "Self reliance," in *Selected Essays*, Penguin Books, 1982.

Evans, Richard and Price, Colin (1999) *Vertical Take-off*, Nicholas Brealey Publishing.

Fenster, Julie M. (2000) *In the Words of the Great Business Leaders*, John Wiley.

Frankl, Viktor E. (1959) *Man's Search for Meaning*, Beacon Press.

Freemantle, David (1995) *79/80 Things You Must Do to be a Great Boss*, McGraw-Hill.

Gianetti, Eduardo (2000) *The Lies We Live By*, Bloomsbury.

Gibbs, Randy J. (1998) *20/20 Insight*, Daybreak.

Gladwell, Malcolm (2000) *The Tipping Point*, Little, Brown & Co.

Gleick, James (1988) *Chaos*, Heinemann.

Goleman, Daniel (1996) *Emotional Intelligence*, Bloomsbury.

Goleman, Daniel (1998) *Working with Emotional Intelligence*, Bloomsbury.

Greenfeld, Karl Taro (1999) "Life on the edge," *Time Magazine*, 6 September.

Harvey-Jones, John (1988) *Making It Happen*, Collins.

Kanter, Rosabeth Moss (1984) *The Change Masters*, Allen & Unwin.

Keenan, Brian (1992) *An Evil Cradling*, Hutchinson.

Khalsa, Dharma Singh (1997) *Brain Longevity*, Century.

Kunde, Jesper (2000) *Corporate Religion*, FT Prentice Hall.

Lewin, Roger and Regine, Birute (1999) *The Soul at Work*, Orion Books.

Madoff, Steven Henry (1999) "Shock for shock's sake," *Time Magazine*, October.

Mandela, Nelson (1994) *The Long Walk to Freedom*, Little, Brown & Co.

Manning, Jeff (1999) *GOT MILK?*, Prima Publishing.

McGregor, Douglas (1966) *Leadership and Motivation*, MIT Press.

McLuhan, Marshall (1994) *Understanding Media*, MIT Press.

Nørretranders, Tor (1998) *The User Illusion*, Penguin Books.

O'Shea, James and Madigan, Charles (1997) *Dangerous Company*, Nicholas Brealey Publishing.

Pearce, Garth (2000) "The talented Mr Minghella," *The Sunday Times*, 9 January.

Peel, M. (1987) *Customer Service*, Kogan Page.

Pert, Candace B. (1997) *Molecules of Emotion*, Scribner.

Peters, Tom (1992) *Liberation Management*, A. Knopf.

Pinker, Steven (1999) *Words and Rules*, Weidenfeld & Nicolson.

Quinn, Robert E. (1996) *Deep Change*, Jossey-Bass.

Richer, Julian (1995) *The Richer Way*, EMAP Business Communications.

Schultz, Howard (1997) *Pour Your Heart Into It*, Hyperion.

Sculley, John (1987) *Odyssey*, Collins.

Senge, Peter (1990) *The Fifth Discipline*, Doubleday.

Sherman, Howard and Schultz, Ron (1998) *Open Boundaries*, Perseus Books.

Simpson, Joe (1988) *Touching the Void*, Jonathan Cape.

Skynner, Robin and Cleese, John (1993) *Life and How to Survive It*, Methuen.

Tillett, A., Kempner, T. and Wills G. (eds) (1970) *Management Thinkers*, Penguin Books.

Tracy, Brian (1998) *Success is a Journey*, Executive Excellence Publishing.

Underhill, Paco (1999) *Why We Buy*, Orion Books.

Viney, John (2000) in *The Independent*, 3 May.

Waterhouse, Rosie (2000) "The willpower test," *The Sunday Times*, 9 January.

Whyte, David (1994) *The Heart Aroused*, Doubleday.

Whyte, William H. (1956) *Organization Man*, Simon & Schuster.

Zander, Rosamund Stone and Zander, Benjamin (2000) *The Art of Possibility*, Cambridge, MA: Harvard Business School Press.

# Index